Praise for *Karmic Selling*

"Fabulous insights on being a great human, building success, and enriching your life. Building success with kindness and authenticity—everything in this book rings true. When Stan sold into my organization, he and I built trust, transparency, and friendship. We made a win-win deal and both realized huge value from our collaboration.

Throughout my career, I have had wins and losses; learning, developing, and building competency on that journey. *Karmic Selling* does work, and success is born in helping people solve problems. This book lays the foundation for successfully solving other people's problems and achieving greater life enrichment."

—RICHARD WARD,
Former Senior Vice President, Baker Hughes

"I've learned some great lessons from Stan over the years, and I'm very excited to see he put all of his thoughts and ideas into a book so that everyone can learn his valuable lessons on how we can conduct ourselves in both our corporate and personal lives in order to achieve greatness.

In every page of this book, you can see Stan's passion for approaching every situation with a 'clean heart.' The case studies are very relatable, as well as Stan's openness about his own life experiences. No matter what type of job you have, we are always selling, and Stan lays the foundation for how to be truly genuine and achieve success."

—STEPHEN LAZAR, JR.,
Fortune 1000 Operations Director

"Like Stan, I had a near-death experience that began a better life. Mine was at sea rather than the road, but it granted me similar epiphanies on work and relationships. The world needs more leaders with a how-can-I-help mindset, so I'm hopeful Stan's book will inspire more paradigm shifts with less dramatic catalysts!

Stan's story reminds us about integrity—doing what's right when no one is looking—and the value and rewards of servant leadership. Humble authenticity in a leader is the strongest magnet for building successful, high-performing teams of leaders, and *Karmic Selling* delivers the proof points in rapid succession.

At home, at work, in all relationships, helping others is its own reward—and sometimes, as *Karmic Selling* demonstrates, it can take us places we only imagined."

— **WAYNE LUCERNONI**, President Government Solutions, Global Engineering Company

"I enjoyed *Karmic Selling* immensely! It is especially applicable for physician executives who, although skilled at communicating with patients, are under-prepared for establishing rewarding business relationships and interacting with administrative executives. The same is true for other professionals with a scientific background, such as engineers and IT experts, when promoted into positions offering services to other business enterprises. This book will help a wide variety of professionals—I plan to purchase copies for my entire leadership team. It's an essential guide to rewarding business relationships."

— **GEORGE WILLIAMS**, MD, Healthcare Executive

"I've known Stan for many years and can personally confirm his approach. When I first met him, the relationship was quite different from anything I had ever experienced from someone 'selling' something to me. What I came to truly appreciate was how he always tried to help me and my company, even when there wasn't a 'sale' to be made—at least at that moment.

Stan's thoughtful guidance works, and not just in business—you can use it to make all the relationships in your life more rewarding."

—STEVE HENDERSON,
Executive Vice President, Leggett & Platt

"Stan's book is a timely reminder about the power of authentic human connection—something many of us have lost touch with. *Karmic Selling* is proof that approaching life with a "however-I-can-help" mindset is the most powerful way to build genuine, long-lasting business relationships and a more fulfilling professional and personal life. Quite frankly, nobody does it better than Stan!"

—PAUL J. TUDOR, CEO, Private Equity

"A must read for everyone, not just the business professional. These are basic principles of making and growing relationships in business and life. The strength of this book is in the case studies and reflection exercises. This is not a read and forget book—apply the principles in your conversations, notes, and follow-ups for an enhanced business and personal life."

—R. KEVIN WELLS, Lecturer,
Auburn University Harbert College of Business

"I could not put it down … *Karmic Selling* is enjoyable, insightful, and engaging. So many themes resonated: a clean heart, helping others, being authentic, and demonstrating credibility. Stan's approaches will benefit people in all aspects of their lives, not just earning business. This book is truly authentic and speaks to Stan's character and desire to help others."

—PATRICK HASTINGS,
Healthcare Executive

"I really enjoyed *Karmic Selling*. Many books explore similar concepts, but this is a more meaningful, personal story. It's not just about successful projects or big wins—it is about people, interactions, and relationships. I've spent my career in supply chain, but the same lessons hold true in my field: be authentic, don't play games, and maintain a 'how can I help' mindset. Stan, thank you for defining a clear way to establish connections and foster long-term relationships founded on trust."

—GIUSEPPE MUZZI,
Fortune 500 Supply Chain Director

"Stan demonstrates that kindness is serious business and proves how successful one can be by valuing the currency of kindness over money."

—MARLY Q CASANOVA,
Kindness Influencer

"Very concise, practical, and in my experience, absolutely the right way to sell."

—BRUCE HOECHNER,
Board Member and Former CEO, Rogers Corporation

"Having been on both sides—consulting as well as leadership positions in the chemical industry—I highly concur with Stan in terms of what works to build long-lasting business relationships that benefit both companies.

Building trust through integrity, competence, authenticity, and perseverance is critical for success. In this book, Stan provides guidelines and examples of how to do this. Knowing Stan now for almost 15 years, I have seen how this has worked for him. His problem-solving approach is contagious for the people he works with and drives success.

As a reader, you can reflect on yourself and determine how you can make this approach work in your own authentic way. And make sure you surround yourself with good people who share your values. Enjoy practicing *Karmic Selling*!"

—BOUDEWIJN VAN LENT,
CEO, VanDeMark Chemical

KARMIC
SELLING

KARMIC SELLING

EARNING BUSINESS
by EARNING TRUST

STAN GWIZDAK

Advantage | Books

Published by Advantage Books, Charleston, South Carolina.
An imprint of Advantage Media.

ADVANTAGE is a registered trademark, and the Advantage colophon is a trademark of Advantage Media Group, Inc.

Printed in the United States of America.

10 9 8 7 6 5 4 3 2 1

ISBN: 978-1-64225-860-8 (Hardcover)
ISBN: 978-1-64225-859-2 (eBook)

Library of Congress Control Number: 2023916169

Cover and layout design by Lance Buckley.

This publication is designed to provide accurate and authoritative information in regard to the subject matter covered. It is sold with the understanding that the publisher is not engaged in rendering legal, accounting, or other professional services. If legal advice or other expert assistance is required, the services of a competent professional person should be sought.

Advantage Books is an imprint of Advantage Media Group. Advantage Media helps busy entrepreneurs, CEOs, and leaders write and publish a book to grow their business and become the authority in their field. Advantage authors comprise an exclusive community of industry professionals, idea-makers, and thought leaders. For more information go to **advantagemedia.com**.

To you, dear reader

"There are no strangers here, only friends you haven't yet met."
—**WILLIAM BUTLER YEATS**, Poet

CONTENTS

I never wanted to be a "sales guy." I've always hated that idea—*that guy*. He's the good-looking guy with the big cheesy smile in the blue leisure suit. He's the kind of person who sells your grandma a lemon on the used car lot and doesn't give a crap that he's just cheated an old lady. That's how I've always seen the "sales guy," and that's not my style. If that resonates with you, keep reading. You don't have to be in sales to get value out of this book. Every day, we are "selling" ourselves in our interactions with others, trying to present ourselves well, be it in business or in our private lives. This book is all about approaching those interactions in an authentic way and living a life that's true to who you are—who you *really* are—as a human being.

As I was thinking about writing this book, I wondered where my negative feeling about sales came from. It started with a door-to-door Kirby Sweeper sales guy. He came into my childhood home with a vacuum cleaner to sell, plus all the snazzy attachments and shiny features. He was smooth, telling my dad how it could take care of almost any work around the house, and could help keep "the Mrs." happy. Dad ended up buying that Kirby Sweeper for an astounding price—about $1,000. This was 1976, so $1,000 was a *lot* of money.

That was way more than we could afford for a vacuum cleaner, and my mom got really pissed. I remember them arguing about it. The sales guy made his sale, but he sure did wreck our household for a while. And, by the way, we never painted our car, used the sanding option, or tried any of the other features that came with that Sweeper. We just used it to clean the floor. That was when I personally saw how compelling but untrustworthy a "sales guy" could be.

We all have a story like that—the time we got swindled by a slick sales pitch or a high-pressure salesperson. And yet, here I am, writing a book about sales. But I still don't consider myself a "sales guy." What gives?

First, the era of "the sales guy" is dead; nobody wants to feel like they're being sold to these days. People want authentic connection. They want to be seen. They want to be heard. They want to know *how you can help them.* And they want help from someone they can trust.

> *It's all about approaching each meeting with a clean heart, connecting with the other person, and asking them, what can I do for you?*

That's what I've built my career on: prioritizing how I can help others and earning their trust. It's worked for me, most of the time, and I'm confident it can work for you, too. It's all about approaching each meeting with a clean heart, connecting with the other person, and asking them, *what can I do for you?*

I call it Karmic Selling. The term karmic has roots in Hinduism, Buddhism, and Jainism. While I don't belong to these religious traditions, the notion that doing good comes back to you always resonated with me. In the pages that follow, I'll explain exactly what I mean by "Karmic Selling" and give you actionable steps on how to make it work for you. But first, you probably want to know:

how did a non-sales-guy end up writing a book about sales? Like I said, I never identified as "the sales guy." But much of my career has involved sales, whether that meant selling myself, selling a product, or selling a service. That said, the "selling" was usually done in a less traditional way. In truth, I haven't been a sales guy so much as I've been a "solutions guy."

How It All Started: A BB Gun

I could start by telling you about what I achieved in my career at companies like Goodyear Tire, General Electric (GE), Honeywell, or Textron. But the truth is, my career started *way* before that. It started with a BB gun.

I was a kid, growing up in Carrolltown, Pennsylvania, about two hours east of Pittsburgh. That town spanned an area of two miles. It had one church, one stop light, and seven bars. Even today, the population is less than 1,000—some 850 people as of February 2023. Needless to say, it was the kind of town where everybody knew everybody. You couldn't get away with anything. If you were a kid acting out of line, and your parents weren't around to smack some sense into you, another parent would oblige.

Growing up, our family didn't have a whole lot of money. I had three younger brothers and one older sister, and if any of us kids wanted something, we had to work for it. When I was about nine or ten, most of my buddies had a BB gun. So, I wanted one, too. But my parents weren't buying me one, so I'd have to find my own way.

I saw an ad in the back of a magazine promoting an opportunity to sell plant seeds door to door with American Seed Company—and I saw my chance. The company sent the first box of seeds for free, and I started selling. I sold out, sent them the money I owed, ordered some more, kept selling—and sold out again. The neighbors trusted me, and I became the little seed peddler.

Even at that age, I started implementing practices I still use today. I figured out that it made sense to take notes about each house: the name of the person, the type of seeds they bought, and how many. I knew that Mrs. Jones wanted tulip bulbs and Mr. Rogers wanted zucchinis. I kept those notes and, the next year, I knew exactly what each person wanted and had it ready for them—and I had some ideas for what *else* they might want. Maybe Mrs. Jones could add some roses to her flowerbed, or Mr. Rogers could add some cucumbers to his vegetable garden. I was forecasting and upselling without realizing what either was.

That was my first foray into the business world. It taught me a lesson I still use today—and that I'll talk about in detail later (see chapter 8, all about the value of note-taking). Taking notes about someone when you meet them and remembering professional and personal facts helps establish a rapport—and that's what I'm all about: connecting with people.

I didn't know it back then (I just wanted my BB gun), but I was already learning that by taking the time to get to *know* people—their names, their gardens, what kind of flowers they liked—I could succeed. I was already learning the power of genuine connection. I was laying the groundwork for my future approach to sales: Karmic Selling. And for those who are wondering: yep, I got my BB gun.

From then on, I had odd jobs throughout school and college, where I studied mechanical engineering. One of my favorite gigs during college was working on a road crew. I was that "Stop" sign guy, getting cars to slow down as they approached a construction site. I'd get so bored, I'd be dancing with the sign, waving to people, striking up conversations with them—again, what I didn't realize then, but I see now, is that it was all about connecting with people.

The Corporate Disappointments Start Stacking Up

I graduated from Penn State with my mechanical engineering degree in 1989. At the time, I was ready to take on the corporate world, eager, and optimistic. I didn't have a clue what was coming my way. I ended up working for Goodyear, starting out in the purchasing department. Later, I put my degree to use working in a tire mold manufacturing plant in Stow, Ohio, as an engineer. In my first supervisory role, I had six people reporting to me. By the time I was in my mid-twenties, I was in charge of seventy-five people.

So, I was making my way up the ladder. Great, right? Not quite. I was already seeing parts of the corporate world that weren't sitting right with me. This was a time when corporations were still very "traditional." There was no talk of employee wellness, pay transparency, or diversity and inclusion like today. So, when I say corporate, I'm talking about that antagonistic, competitive, bureaucratic kind of culture. "Corporate" itself doesn't have to be bad. There are plenty of great corporations these days that are renowned for fantastic cultures and corporate citizenship. I'm sure there were companies getting it right back then, too. But my experience was a bit different, so I started experiencing some corporate disappointments—tiny cracks in that glossy corporate façade that gave way over time.

Here's one: I remember watching the plant manager come in every day, walk past me and the 150 folks doing the dirty work without a word, and go to his office. At the end of the day, he'd come back out of his office, walk by us all—again without saying a thing—and leave. That got me kind of sour. I'm the kind of person who likes to communicate with people. His dismissive attitude felt wrong.

Other times, the corporate attitudes weren't just dismissive. They were downright rude, insulting, or demeaning. I'll never forget the call I had with my boss fifteen days after I'd stepped into a VP/GM role of a business unit. I'm paraphrasing, but his words were along the lines of, "If you f-ing guys don't start f-ing making your f-ing numbers, I'm going to f-ing shut you down. Do you f-ing understand me?" The thing was, I had no clue what he was talking about—because we'd *made* our "f-ing" numbers. When I calmly pointed that out, the call mysteriously got "disconnected."

I told myself that one day I'd run my own plant, and I'd do things differently. And I felt ready to take that step, but every time the topic of me running my own plant came up, I was shuffled to the side. The message I got was, "You're too young. Get some gray hairs, and *then* we'll talk."

I was impatient and eager to get ahead. So, when I still wasn't running my own plant at Goodyear after seven years, and I got a chance to interview with GE, I jumped on it. In that interview, I asked them, "When can I run my own plant?" Their answer was a breath of fresh air. They didn't go on about age or experience. They just said, "When you prove to us that you can." I went for it.

I ended up staying with GE for a good while. I started out as a Six Sigma Black Belt and got promoted a year later, to a Master Black Belt. A year after that, I was promoted to an internal vice president role of a business unit. And then, shortly after that, I was named president of a newly acquired business that GE Aircraft Engines purchased: Turbine Metal Technology (TMT).

Over those GE years, I learned *a lot*, starting with the Six Sigma process. As I fine-tuned the craft of Lean manufacturing, I made process improvements—and those improvements got me noticed. I generated productivity gains of $12.1 million from 1996 to 1999 using Lean/Six Sigma. I increased operating margins by 28 percent in 1999, and 811 percent in 2000. And I improved on-time delivery to customers by 34 percent in 1998 and 51 percent in 2000. But those are just numbers, and numbers don't make for a fulfilling career.

The further up the ladder I got, the more I learned about the corporate world—and more of those corporate disappointments started adding up. The whole time, I was trying to prove, *I have what it takes to run my own plant.* Remember, that had been my goal since I started and was part of the reason that I left Goodyear. Chasing that dream, I moved for work—dragging my poor wife with me from Peebles, Ohio, to McAllen, Texas.

Then, I got the president's position with TMT, and I was asked to move to the California area. My wife was nearly due to give birth to our first daughter and not in a position to move. So, I told my boss, "Hey, my wife is pregnant. She's going to give birth in about four weeks. Can I stay here with my wife and work that job from here for now? I can fly out there, but I want to fly back to be with her." His response? "If you want the job, get your ass out there." Off I went.

When our daughter was born, I flew back to Texas to be with her and my wife. I stayed one day and then flew back to California. That was it. If I wanted to keep my job, I didn't have a choice. Losing those first precious days of family connection was another one of those corporate disappointments. I realized that the elite business world that I'd been so eager to join wasn't as great as I'd thought. I started eyeing the exits. But it would take a much bigger shock—a life-or-death situation, literally—for me to finally break out of the corporate rat race.

The Breaking Point

Clearly, the corporate world is right for many people. It offers more stability and certainty than striking out on your own. However, I was realizing that the traditional corporate world wasn't quite right for me. Still, I kept on. I was climbing that corporate ladder with my blinders on. I shifted from GE to Honeywell, working in their aerospace services division—which is where I was when 9/11 happened. Our business was paused almost immediately. I had to lay off about 30 percent of our people and barely survived the cuts myself.

To this day, I call that the darkest point of my career. Knowing that the people I worked with were now facing the question of, "How do I pay the bills? How do I put food on the table for my kids? What's next?" was bad enough. Being the person who had to break the news to them made it that much worse. The horrible circumstances that led to the whole scenario left a lot of us feeling helpless and out of control.

From Honeywell, I transitioned to a series of other roles and companies, always with a focus on process improvement. My work took me from Akron and Peebles Ohio, to McAllen, Texas, Oregon, South Carolina, Nashville, and—finally—Charlotte, North Carolina. I wasn't just running in the rat race; I was *sprinting* the whole damn time. I'm talking sleepless nights, high blood pressure, and constant stress. I couldn't give my family the time and attention I wanted. I was barely taking care of myself, let alone anybody else. Maybe you've been there and know how awful it is.

Then, I got the wakeup call. On November 17, 2004, at 11:17 a.m., I was in a car accident. A bad one. *That* was the turning point, and I'll talk about it more in the next chapter. That was the moment when I finally asked myself, "What the *heck* are you doing with your life?" That was the moment when I decided I was tired of clawing my way up the ladder—and that, instead, I wanted to focus on helping people and connecting with them. It was the moment I decided to approach life—both professionally and personally—as my authentic self.

That mindset shift was pivotal for my career. I left my corporate job shortly after the accident and started my own consultancy with a fresh point of view. I finally understood that sales didn't have to mean putting on that blue leisure suit and a fake smile and giving someone the big "Here's why you should buy from me" shtick.

I finally *got it*: the key to my success had always been, and will always be, connection. Over time, I came to name my approach "Karmic Selling." It's all about putting others' needs before your own and establishing an authentic rapport with them. That's the kind of connection that leaves people (and you) feeling *good* and makes them want to keep in touch with you. Sometimes, that may even mean they want to do business with you.

> *The key to my success had always been, and will always be, connection.*

In this book, I lay out the principles of Karmic Selling for you, because I'm hoping it can help you find greater success in your life. Yes, this is a sales book. But it's also a personal book about the power of human connection and about how connectivity benefits us as humans, personally and professionally.

If you look up sales books on Amazon, you'll find thousands of how-to guides: step-by-step plans for "generating leads," special formulas "to increase sales by 25 percent," and tips for "closing the deal." I don't want to talk about any of that stuff. For me, it's not about a formula. It's about being true to your own purpose and authentic self. This book talks about how I got there and gives some pointers for how you can get there, but the aim isn't to make you a copy of me.

Instead, I hope this book helps you believe two things:

1. *I can succeed by being authentic and kind.*
2. *Success begins with asking the question, "How can I help you?"*

Those are the core principles of Karmic Selling. If you stick to those principles, you're bound to do what's right—and good karma will come back to you as a result. You'll find that when you put good out into the world, you'll get it back tenfold. I firmly believe that, because I've seen it happen time and again.

You can be successful while embracing authenticity and being true to yourself—and straightforward with others. Authenticity in the business world isn't always easy, especially when find yourself in a rat race, striving for success. There's nothing wrong with wanting success. Karmic Selling can help you find it while serving others—instead of stepping on others to get to the top.

"When you truly understand karma, then you realize you are responsible for everything in your life. It is incredibly empowering to know that your future is in your hands."

—**KEANU REEVES,** actor

"When you carry out acts of kindness, you get a wonderful feeling inside. It is as though something inside your body responds and says, yes, this is how I ought to feel."

—**HAROLD KUSHNER,**
rabbi, author, and lecturer

CHAPTER 1

The Shift

Most days in life go by in a blur. We don't remember each one. For me, there's a few I'll never forget: the day I met my wife; the day we got married; the days my kids were born. And the day I almost died.

It was 2004. I was working a corporate job in Charlotte, North Carolina, lost in the rat race. I'd already seen some success in my career, with experience at companies like Goodyear, GE, and Honeywell. But I'd also seen plenty of those corporate disappointments I mentioned, and I already had some idea that I wanted *out*—that the rat race wasn't for me.

On that day, I was racing to a meeting in my little Mazda Miata, listening to *Rich Dad, Poor Dad*, by Robert T. Kiyosaki, as I drove. Already, I was looking for inspiration and guidance, trying to figure out my exit strategy—but not yet ready to take the leap. What happened next would change that.

As I was driving, I realized I was going to be late. So, I reached for my cell phone, planning to let the team know. For just a second, I took my eyes off the road. When I looked back up, a big rig had pulled out in front of me. It had a trailer hitched to it, carrying some huge cement slabs. My tiny car didn't stand a chance.

In a split second, I weighed my options. I could go left, into oncoming traffic. I could go right, into a huge ditch. Or I could go straight. I made my choice, slammed on the brakes, and went straight. I unbuckled my seatbelt so I could lay down across the passenger seat, and I remember saying "Oh my God" and bringing my hands up to my face as I ducked down. Peeking through my fingers, the last thing I saw was the windshield glass breaking, crumpling into the car, and shattering—I still have scars on my fingers from the glass.

Then, I blacked out—for which I am very thankful. I came to with an emergency team loading me into a chopper. I distinctively remember feeling the wind from the blades on my face and hearing that *woosh, woosh* of the rotors above me. A woman asked me "Where do you hurt?" At that point, I realized pretty much *everything* hurt. I passed out again—but not before hearing the woman say, "Alright boys, cut off his clothes."

When I woke up again, I was in the hospital. I came to because of the pain: a nurse was soaking my hands and scrubbing them with what felt like steel wool, trying to remove any remaining shards of windshield from the cuts in my hands. My wife was there—pregnant with our second daughter, and in her ninth month. I remember her joking with the team that they might have to attend to her next. I was in a heck of a lot of pain, mostly from the broken ribs.

But I was alive.

I walked out of the hospital twenty-four hours later. Of course, my boss told me to take some time off to recover, which I did. And that left me some time to think about what the heck had just happened to me. It was November of 2004. Our second daughter was born two weeks later, while I was still in bandages. In July 2005, I left the corporate world, determined to do things differently.

The aftermath of my collision with a big rig. This moment changed my life forever.

That is what it took for me to change. Your path to change doesn't need to be that dramatic. You don't need a car wreck, health scare, or trauma of any kind to shift your thinking. You can shift it on your own—and it all starts with dropping what I like to call the "f— you" chip on your shoulder. The "f— you" chip can serve as an aggressive shield or cloak required for survival in toxic environments. That's the first step in switching from a success-at-all-costs mindset to a however-I-can-help mindset, an attitude that prioritizes connection over selling, serving over self.

And that sets into motion the laws of karma—the laws that dictate that, by genuinely seeking to connect with and help other people, you will put out good karma and, before long, that positive karma will come back to you. And it will come back to you tenfold, I promise you. Just watch.

Goodbye to the "F— You" Chip

Before the crash, I was sometimes your stereotypical corporate jerk. My goal was climbing the corporate ladder. That's all I was focused on—to become "The Man," capital T, capital M. I wanted to be the top dog, and damned be anything and anyone that got in my way. I had this idea that if *I* didn't grab it—the deal, the promotion, the money—someone else would. It was a stressful way to go through life.

At the same time, I was secretly fed up with the corporate disappointments. I'd seen the power grabs, the betrayals, the nepotism, and the lies that people used to get ahead. I'd become disillusioned with the "corporate hangers-on," the people who don't give a crap if they do a *good* job, but just do the bare minimum. But still, I was clinging to that "f— you chip." After all, it had worked for me so far. I'd gotten promoted, time and again. Whether I was happy or not was another story.

That's what the crash changed for me. I looked back at my life and realized I'd spent most of it working. Not only that, I'd spent most of my working days wearing a corporate mask, clinging to a jackass persona that wasn't true to who I was. I'd spent the majority of my days being totally inauthentic to who I was and what I valued. When I got home from work at the end of each day, I'd literally remind myself to remove the "f— you" chip from my shoulder before I saw my wife and kids. Maybe you've had to do that, too. It's exhausting. It's even worse if you forget to remove it some days.

The car wreck was what it took to get me to drop the chip. I realized my life could've been done right then and there, and I'd spent most of it being someone I wasn't. So, I threw away the chip. It has never come out again. Since then, I've committed myself to authenticity and to what I call a "clean heart." When I say that, I'm not referring to purity or perfection, just good intentions and honesty. I don't have to be somebody else to succeed. I can be myself—and "myself" is a person who seeks connections with people and enjoys presenting them with solutions. By helping other people find solutions, I put some of that good karmic energy I mentioned out into the world, and I find it coming back to me, again and again, as you'll see from the examples to follow.

Approaching People with a Clean Heart Works

So, what do you do when you drop the "f— you" chip? In my case, it means approaching people with good intentions. That means that I go into every interaction with genuine interest, attention, and care. I take the time to get to know people before I meet them, and I listen to them and—if they care to share them—hear their problems. Then, I strive to give them solutions to those problems.

Those solutions aren't necessarily coming from me or my business, and the other person can take those solutions or leave them. The point isn't whether we close a deal, or they take my advice, or follow up on the lead I give them. The point is that I go into the interaction with a genuine desire to help—with a clean heart. I come away from it feeling good and, for the most part, so does the other person. Here are a few examples to prove my point.

Every Detail Counts, Even a Jeep

Before I dropped the "f— you" chip, I often went into business meetings seeing people as dollar signs. I remember going into a meeting for a huge contract early in my career—we're talking millions. All I could think of during that meeting was how much money was at stake. I was looking at the guy in front of me and basically picturing dollar signs over his head as I pitched him. I was feeding him a sales pitch that had nothing to do with him, telling him "Here's why *we're* great… Here's why you need to hire *us*." I basically spewed sales arguments all over him—instead of being present, listening, and meeting him where he needed to be met.

It didn't go well. Big fail. I'd fed him the standard shtick, and after a few minutes, he gave me the standard reply, "I'll call you if I need your services." That was that. Because he could tell that I didn't give a damn about him or his company or his company's problems. I just cared about closing a seven-figure deal. Treating people like dollar signs doesn't work. They want to be treated like *people*. On that occasion, I got it wrong.

Another fail comes from a time when I was working at a Goodyear mold plant, with seventy-five folks reporting to me. This was back in the day when supervisors and employees all wore the same outfit: dark blue pants and a light blue shirt, with your name on one side and the name of your plant on the other. Before I moved to the mold plant, I'd been working up the street at a Goodyear model shop—basically a support shop for the tire mold plant— where I'd had just six folks reporting to me. I'd bridged the gap between management and the union on scheduling issues, which they'd appreciated—and that gratitude would come back to me tenfold, as you'll see.

When I made the jump from managing not six but seventy-five employees, my uniform was the least of my worries. So, I was still wearing my uniform that had the "Goodyear Model Shop" badge instead of the "Goodyear Mold Plant" badge stitched on it. It wasn't a big deal to me, but a guy at the mold plant kept bothering me about getting "Model Shop" off my shirt and changing to a mold-plant uniform. One day, when I was a couple of weeks into this new supervisory role, he came up to me, ripped the "Model Shop" badge off my shirt and told me, "Now you can become one of us."

Under a lot of stress as a new leader, I blew up. Thinking only of myself, I said things that nearly led the two of us out to the parking lot. He gave me my badge back and apologized. But an hour later, the union steward came to see me in my office. The guy I'd threatened had told the union about our altercation. They told me that they'd spoken to him, and he'd agreed not to press charges. They were going to drop it. Why? The union steward had talked to the folks I'd worked with previously—the six guys at the model shop. *Those* guys had vouched for me. They'd said, "Stan's a good guy." They saved me. But it was a close call.

That was early on in my career, when I was more concerned with getting to the top than approaching the world with authenticity. I was young and hot-headed, and I behaved in a way that embarrasses me today. Again: I got it very wrong that day. Later in my career, my attitude shifted, and I started to get it right.

On one occasion, I had a first meeting with a potential client. I did my research as part of my meeting prep—a process I'll discuss in detail in chapter 4—and learned that she was an ex-GE employee, like me. When we met, I brought up her GE past; that broke the ice. It even turned out that we had a mutual acquaintance at GE.

The link got us talking. And then we talked about *everything*, from our kids to our cars. She mentioned that she had an old Jeep she was trying to sell—actually, it was her husband's old Jeep that *he* was trying to sell, and she was pretty pissed that it was still sitting in their driveway. It was this small detail, something that might seem inconsequential to anyone else, but I wrote it down in my meeting notes: *Trying to sell hubby's Jeep. Vintage model.*

Afterward, my boss asked me: "Stan, why the heck did you make a note about a Jeep?" He didn't think it was important because it wasn't business. But I could see that it mattered to *her*, so I figured it should matter to me.

In my follow-up email after our first meeting, I came back to it. I was also a Jeep-owner—a 1973 Jeep CJ-5—and I had connections to the Jeep community. I had some ideas on how she might sell the vehicle, which I shared in my follow-up email: "Hey, you mentioned you're trying to unload a Jeep. Those vintage models are pretty popular. You could even try Craigslist. Here's some other resources that can help." It was totally unrelated to our business conversation; I had no agenda, other than to help this woman get that Jeep out of her driveway.

That's when her attitude shifted. She mentally took a step back as she realized, "This guy is for real. He listened to me, and he brought me a solution. He didn't even try to sell me." That little detail ultimately led to us working together. While my bosses expected my meeting notes to focus only on the business side of things, I knew the personal side was just as important. It was the key to my connection with her—and that connection is what made her want to work with me. In fact, when I left that consulting role a few months later, the client left with me, because her connection was with me, not with the consulting firm.

Karma Is Real—and Often Found in Airports

Now, those moments of trying to do some good for others aren't limited to professional settings. In fact, one of the most powerful examples I have of that karmic however-I-can-help mindset coming back tenfold comes from my personal life.

I was in the Pittsburgh Airport, checking into the swanky airport lounge. The guy in front of me couldn't get in; he thought he had access but didn't, for whatever reason, and they told him it was sixty bucks for a one-day pass or something like that. So, he said, "forget it" and was getting ready to walk off. I stepped forward and introduced myself to the team behind the check-in counter. I pointed to the guy, who was still there, and said, "I'm so sorry, I should have introduced myself sooner. He's my guest today."

Now, those moments of trying to do some good for others aren't limited to professional settings.

I wasn't fooling anybody. Clearly, I didn't know this guy. But the team behind the check-in counter played ball and checked us both in. We got into the club, and I told him, "Hey man, have a great day. Enjoy." I wasn't expecting anything from him. I just saw the opportunity to help, so I did. He asked me how he could pay me back and I told him, "Just pay it forward." He said, "Okay." Case closed.

Then we started chatting, and he told me he was a urologist, specializing in prostate cancer. By coincidence, I had a guy on my team who had just been diagnosed with prostate cancer. So, I told him, "Look, I didn't have any kind of agenda when I got you in here, and you don't have to do this. There's no hook. The thing is, a guy on my team was just diagnosed with prostate cancer. And he's got questions. Would you mind talking to him about his options?"

He agreed, and we exchanged numbers on the spot. What are the odds? I had no clue what that guy did for a living when I got him into the lounge. But he was exactly the expert someone on my team needed. Right place, right time. It's those moments when I think, "Karma is real."

Approaching People with a Clean Heart Feels Good

I could give you a thousand more examples of times when I've approached an interaction with a clean heart and came away all the better for it, but this book has a word limit. I do want to point out one more thing about those interactions—and it's that they feel *good*.

When you do or say something nice to someone, or help them in some way, you get a warm fuzzy feeling, and it's freaking *awesome*. The Harold Kushner quote at the start says it better than I can: "When you carry out acts of kindness, you get a wonderful feeling inside. It is as though something inside your body responds and says, yes, this is how I ought to feel."

Right on.

I know that *this-is-how-I-ought-to-feel* mood. It happened to me recently, at a grocery store. It was something small: I complimented a woman on her hair. She had this really striking hairstyle, with all these colorful braids. You could tell she put some time into it. I thought, *Wow, that's kind of cool.* I hesitated to say something, because I didn't want her to take it the wrong way or think I was some kind of grocery store creep. Then I figured, *Look, I'm approaching this with good intentions, and she'll see that.* So, I told her, "Hey, I really love your hair."

This woman turned around with the biggest smile on her face. She told me she'd gotten her hair done for her birthday, and nobody in her family had said anything—she seemed pretty disappointed about it. But she was so happy someone had appreciated her effort, even if that someone was a total stranger. We started chatting, and she asked if she could give me a hug. We ended up hugging it out and just had this moment of awesome, authentic connectivity.

If you've ever given (or received) a compliment, you probably know that warm-and-fuzzy feeling. It's not bullshit. There's science to back it up. Research has shown that compliments make people feel *great*—in fact, usually the compliment-giver underestimates just how good their words will make the compliment-receiver feel. On top of that, the same research suggests that the person *giving* the compliment feels good as a result too. It's a reciprocal deal. Everyone's a winner.[1,2]

Some studies even suggest that receiving a compliment is as good as getting paid. In one study, subjects' brain activity was monitored via functional magnetic resonance imaging as they received a monetary reward versus a social reward (a compliment). The results? Receiving a compliment activated the same parts of the brain as when a person was given a monetary reward.[3]

When I say that approaching people with a clean heart is worth it, I've got the science to back it up. A simple compliment is just one basic example of how approaching the world with a clean heart reaps rewards. You get that endorphin rush right away. So, who's to say that a clean heart can't reap rewards in the business world too? In my experience, it sure can.

1   Erica J. Boothby and Vanessa K. Bohns, "Why a Simple Act of Kindness Is Not as Simple as It Seems: Underestimating the Positive Impact of Our Compliments on Others," *Personality and Social Psychology Bulletin* 47, no. 5 (2021): 826–840, https://doi.org/10.1177/0146167220949003.

2   Abigail Fagan, "The psychology of compliments: A nice word goes a long way," *Psychology Today*, September 14, 2021, https://www.psychologytoday.com/us/blog/evidence-based-living/202109/the-psychology-compliments-nice-word-goes-long-way.

3   Keise Izuma, Daisuke N. Saito, and Norihiro Sadato, "Processing of Social and Monetary Rewards in the Human Striatum," *Neuron* 58, no. 2 (2008): 284–294, https://doi.org/10.1016/j.neuron.2008.03.020.

How to Bring a Clean Heart to Business

Approaching people with a clean heart is awesome in any context, be it business or personal. Figuring out how to bring that clean-heart approach to the corporate world isn't always easy, though. I mean, you can't just go around giving people compliments during meetings. But you can go into every meeting with your helper hat on. Instead of thinking, "What can this person do for me?" think "What can I do for this person?"

> *Approaching people with a clean heart is awesome in any context, be it business or personal.*

If you don't have an answer right away, don't stress. Sometimes, you can get an idea of how to help the person while you're doing your prep work. Other times, you'll figure it out when you're listening to them during the meeting. When I say "listen," I mean *actually* listen. Ask questions, probe, and take notes. Taking notes helps you remember what they tell you—even the small details, like the fact that they have a Jeep they're trying to sell.

Your actions after that meeting make a difference too. I walk around with a roll of stamps and some cheap cards from Walgreen's in my pocket, so I can drop thank-you notes in the mail after any meeting I have. I don't try to sell them in that note; I just say *thank you*. Follow-through is another major point. Do what you say you're going to do. If you tell them you're going to send them a presentation tonight, send it tonight. Don't wait till tomorrow. Always deliver on your commitments.

Take the clean-heart approach and you'll see success. You'll see how you can sell without being the "sales guy" in the same leisure blue suit all the other sales guys wear. It's an approach that anyone who's willing to embrace authenticity can take. I know, because I've watched other people adopt it and succeed. Case in point: Mike Smith.

CASE STUDY

Mike Smith (Vice President of Research and Development, Desert Tech)

Mike Smith is the perfect example of the fact that you don't have to be a "sales guy" to sell. We met while I was still developing my Karmic Selling philosophy, and he was an early adoptee. I'll let him tell you how it went.

I always felt that salespeople in general were fake—like they were playing an angle. It was always an angle that pretended to be customer focused, but it was really focused on making the sale, and I didn't like that.

I told Stan when we first started working together, "I'm not a sales guy. If that's what you're looking for, then I won't be successful in this position." But Stan already had the beginnings of his Karmic Selling philosophy at that time, and he told me, "Mike, I don't want you to be a sales guy." So, we connected on that. We approached relationships similarly: it's about getting to know the individual and their pain point.

One of the first projects Stan and I worked together was for a client in oil and gas. That's a tough field—there's a lot of money at stake, and they don't like fakes. You're either in the club or you're out. This company had a big project in Mexico that wasn't going well. We came along and, at first, we faced some distrust from the person in the company with whom we were working. But we spent a lot of time talking to them and asking them not only about the project but also about their own goals: "What is it that you want to get out of this? What will help you the most? What happens for you if this project goes badly? What happens if it goes right?"

And by taking the time to talk to them, we won their trust and we found the right ways to help them. I think we wound up doing about $5 million in contracts with them. The person we worked with was happy, and he ended up moving up the ladder after that, because the higher-ups were happy too.

A Clean Heart: The Core of Karmic Selling

The car wreck led me to want more. It's when I decided to lean into this new, freeing mindset—embracing authenticity and prioritizing doing good. I wanted to help people no matter what, whether they would bring me business (and profits) or not. I wanted to build a network, a community of sorts, where I came into every business scenario with pure intentions.

That was the mindset I brought with me when I started my own business in 2005. I ditched the "f— you" chip, and I made sure my company reflected that. I've been running my own consultancy since 2005 through many changes and evolutions. Through it all, I've had one clear rule: "No assholes allowed."

I don't want jerks on my team, and I don't want to do business with them either. If I see that "f— you" chip on a potential client's shoulder, I'll usually politely bow out, even if it means losing money. I want to do business with a clean heart, and I want to do business with people who share that mindset. I know that I might lose a deal today—but another one, maybe a better one, will come. And that's because I stand by my commitment to being my kind, authentic self.

It wasn't always easy—I've had my moments of doubt, which I'll talk about later—but I eventually came to see that approaching business with kindness and authenticity paid off. I saw that when I put "good" out into the world, I got "good" back.

That realization of how powerful those good intentions can be was critical to developing my however-I-can-help mindset—the basis of what I now call "Karmic Selling." I've carried it with me since, and it's proven incredibly empowering. Like that Keanu Reeves quote at the start of the chapter says, "When you truly understand karma, then you realize you are responsible for everything in your life. It is incredibly empowering to know that your future is in your hands."

I promise you: if you want a great future, living your life with a clean heart is a great start.

REFLECTION EXERCISE
A Clean-Heart Checklist

How can you drop the "f— you" chip and approach business with kindness and authenticity? Here are some ideas:

- *Be ready to help:* Approach every meeting with a however-I-can-help mindset. Instead of thinking, "What can this person do for me?" think "What can I do for this person?" If the person needs info and you have it, send it along! Presentations, studies, even an inspiring quote, can help them. I'll talk more about how to implement this in chapter 2.

- *Be authentic and seek to connect:* Be true to your inner self. Don't try to be something you're not and don't pretend to know something that you do not know. People can feel something is wrong if you aren't being yourself. At the same time, meet the person where they are. Nurture a connection by making a genuine effort to get to know them and understand their problems. This requires cultural, situational, and personal awareness. I'll talk more about this in chapter 3.

- *Prepare before you meet:* Research the person professionally and personally. I'll put in three hours of prep work for a one-hour meeting. I'll go into detail on how to prepare for that first meeting in chapter 4.

- *Listen during the first meeting:* Don't cram sales arguments down their throat. Ask questions. Pinpoint the problem. Do you have a solution? This is your chance to figure out how to help. I talk more about that first meeting, the most important one, in chapter 5.

- *Follow through on first and second meetings:* By the end of your first meeting, you'll ideally have a second meeting set—or at least a follow-up date. If there's nothing you can do for that person now, maybe you can do something for them later. Keep your promises and follow through. I discuss the second, third, and subsequent meetings in chapter 6.

- *Keep the conversation flowing:* Stay true to who you are. Don't embellish or misrepresent yourself. If you don't know, you don't know. Honesty is important. People can sniff out a fake. I talk about these conversations in chapter 7.

- *Take notes:* Taking notes lets you remember what the person tells you—even the small details, like the fact that they have a Jeep they're trying to sell. I talk more about note-taking in chapter 8.

- *Follow up:* Say thank you. I mention this above, but I'm going to say it again because it's one of the most important points. *Say thanks.* Someone gave you their time, energy, and attention. Show your gratitude. Chapter 9 is all about follow-up.

- *Be prepared to adapt and grow:* People change. Businesses change. Situations change. Unprecedented events, like global pandemics, occur. Always be ready to adapt. Growing a circle of supportive business friends will help you through the shifts. Chapter 10 addresses this point.

"I've learned that people will forget what you said, people will forget what you did, but people will never forget how you made them feel."

—**MAYA ANGELOU,** author, poet, and civil rights activist

CHAPTER 2

However
I Can Help

Throughout my career, I've often met people with crossed arms. The skeptics. The wary. They're thinking "Hey, you wanna sell me something? Good luck." In those conversations, I've always had one goal—get them to uncross their arms.

When I talk about "crossed arms," I don't mean just physically. Many people come at me with *mentally* crossed arms. I can see from their attitude, expressions, or words that they don't trust me. They think I'm like that Kirby Sweeper sales guy who screwed over my parents. They are guarded and cautious.

In those situations, the solution is always to adopt a however-I-can-help mindset. I'm not coming at them, aggressively pushing them to buy this or that. Instead, I'm aiming to *give* them something—I'm coming in with the mindset of "What help, support, or guidance can I give this person?"

Usually, that gets their arms uncrossed—not right away, because I'm usually met with skepticism at first. People don't believe that you're willing to actually *help* them. But once you win their trust and show them that you're for real, those arms get uncrossed, mentally and physically. I've managed to crack some real tough executives with this approach.

I remember meeting this CEO in Boston, a real hard-charger, fast-talking, in-your-face type of executive. When he met me, his guard was up big time. He'd worked for McKinsey previously and knew how consultants could be: *sell, sell, sell.* He knew that most consultants were coming in and looking at the dollar signs over his head; they just wanted to sell the project and close the deal. So, he was coming from a place of serious doubt. I can't blame him.

When we first met, he was so guarded, he didn't want to let me know how I could help him. He put up a big front and told me everything was great. To boot, he made it clear that if it *wasn't* great, he wasn't going to hire me—he was going to hire his old buddies at McKinsey. He literally told me that in the meeting. The attitude was, "I'm living on cloud nine. I have no issues in my company. But if I do, McKinsey's solving them."

Sounds like a waste of my time, right? Well, I'd done my prep work—an invaluable step, which I'll talk about more in chapter 4—so I knew that everything *wasn't* fine with this company. He wasn't living on cloud nine. I'd looked at the company's financials, and there was a plant down in Virginia that was having some quality issues. So, I asked him about it: "I hear you. Everything is good and peachy. I just happened to see that this one plant might be giving you some headaches. Can you tell me a little bit about that?"

I'd found the sore spot—that plant down in Virginia. At first, he got defensive and crossed his arms. But then we started talking. He'd already had some folks from McKinsey try to fix this plant. No dice. The main issue, it turned out, was a culture problem. He'd cycled through a few general managers trying to fix it, which was just messing up morale more.

Now, to be honest with you, at this point, I really didn't think this guy was going to give me any work. He'd barely given me the time of day to begin with, and now I'd just poked his sore spot about this one plant. He didn't exactly like me.

But the thing was: I had a concrete idea for how to help him. I told him, "Look, we recently did some work for another company with a similar problem—morale issues impacting quality. I've got the report from that job. Let me strip out the name of the company from the report and send it to you. Take your own internal improvement team and see if that information might help you. You've got the people to implement it. Go fix it yourself. I'm sure you've already spent a lot of money on McKinsey, and your board is beating on you for it, saying, 'Hey, you spent the money on McKinsey and got no results.' So, just take that info and implement it internally. You don't need me and my team."

That's when the arms uncrossed—in this case, literally. He relaxed, leaned forward, and goes, "You would send that to me without a bill?" I said, "Yeah. We've already done the work. If this can help you, I'm willing to help you." I didn't care if there was a project for my company or not at that point. I saw a need, and I saw a way to fill that need. All I had to do was share information I already had.

I did what I said I would: I sent him that report (after stripping out any identifying details). A month-and-a-half later, I got a call from the same guy: "Hey, Stan, could you come in and tell me more about that project you folks did? I'm running into some roadblocks." Absolutely. I went to meet with him, and again, I wasn't trying to sell him anything. I was just there to answer his questions. At the end of that meeting, he asked me if he could hire my team to help him out.

I ended up selling him a project. Why? Because I prioritized *helping* the guy—not *selling* him. That's what won his trust. That's what got his arms uncrossed. That's what sealed the deal.

However-I-Can-Help: The Key to Overcoming the Closed Body and Mind

You are going to face crossed arms and closed minds in life, be it in the professional or personal world. Crossed arms are how we defend ourselves—literally. There might even be an evolutionary reason for it. Biologists think that, historically, humans crossed their arms as a means of protecting the body physically.[4] That's translated to the modern world: research into nonverbal communication in psychology shows that crossed arms can mean a person is closed off or feeling defensive.[5]

> *There's nothing wrong with the crossed arms. It's how we protect ourselves.*

Physically, crossed arms are meant to protect us. The same is true mentally. When I say someone has "crossed arms," that may refer to their mindset—closed off and unwilling to engage. That skepticism is a defense mechanism. There are so many scamsters out there today, people often won't believe that you're approaching them with a however-I-can-help mindset. Everybody has their own Kirby vacuum cleaner salesperson worries. And we see stories about

---

4   Susan Blackmore, "Is a person being defensive when they cross their arms?" *BBC Science Focus*, n.d., https://www.sciencefocus.com/the-human-body/is-a-person-being-defensive-when-they-cross-their-arms/.

5   Gretchen N. Foley and Julie P. Gentile, "Nonverbal Communication in Psychotherapy," *Psychiatry (Edgmont)* 7, no. 6 (2010): 38–44, https://www.ncbi.nlm.nih.gov/pmc/articles/PMC2898840/.

scams all the time: Tinder Swindlers, GoFundMe cons, Facebook fakes… The list goes on.

Think about it from the other person's side. The crossed-arms attitude is understandable. It's smart. There's nothing *wrong* with the crossed arms. It's how we protect ourselves. It's not a confrontation or an insult. Approach the person with the crossed-arms attitude with that understanding. A little empathy goes a long way.

Now, you might not always be met by a literal crossed-arm stance. However, you'll still be met with a skeptical look—or you'll be tuned out by someone who's putting in their earbuds, or you'll be questioned outright. Expect the crossed arms in one form or another. Make it your mission to uncross them.

From my experience, the key to overcoming the closed body and mind has always been the however-I-can-help mindset. People don't want to be sold to. But if you can help them—I mean *really* help them, with a tangible problem they're having—you can win their hearts and minds. And best of all, you'll get that warm, fuzzy feeling inside that I mentioned in chapter 1.

However-I-Can-Help Means Helping without an Agenda

I've experienced the however-I-can-help mentality from both sides. I've been the helper, and I've been the person receiving the help. When I was a young manager, early in my career at GE, my boss called me to his office. He told me, "Stan, I like the work you're doing down in McAllen, Texas. And I've got a spot for you to talk to Jim McNerney in our upcoming quality day, where we pitch him some ideas. I want you to talk to him." Now, Jim was a top dog, the CEO of GE Aircraft Engines.

I knew it was a big opportunity. So, I asked my boss, "What do I present?" and he told me, "Put something together around Lean and Six Sigma." Fine. I put together a twenty-page presentation. Quite frankly, it was crap. But I was an eager young kid, trying to make a good impression. Back then, I thought that meant showing *everything* I knew. I wanted to prove to the big boss that I knew my stuff. "Lean and Six Sigma? I'm your guy! Look, I know twenty pages of this stuff!"

Now, anyone who's dealt with some top dogs in the business world knows they value their time more than anything. You don't want to waste the big boss' time. They'll eat you up. I hadn't quite realized that yet. But my boss knew—he knew that if I went in front of Jim with twenty pages worth of crap, Jim would tune me out fast and forget about me even faster.

I gave my boss that twenty-pager to review before the meeting with Jim. He came back to me with one page and said, "*This* is what I want you to present." There was no reason for my boss to do that. It wasn't his job to fix my presentation. He had tons of folks working for him; he didn't have time to fiddle around with someone else's slide deck. Still, he went out of his way to help me.

My boss not only set me up to get face time with one of the senior management folks at GE, he also made sure I didn't screw it up. I appreciated it back then—and, looking back with some more experience under my belt and a few more gray hairs, I appreciate it even more now. That was decades ago, and I still remember that incident.

The Maya Angelou quote at the top of this chapter sums it up: "I've learned that people will forget what you said, people will forget what you did, but people will never forget how you made them feel." My boss made me feel important. He made me feel seen. He made me feel like I had something of value to contribute. There was nothing in it for him; he helped me without an agenda or objective. I've never forgotten it. To this day, if that man came to me for help, I'd do what I could to help him in a second.

I've also been on the other side of the equation and had the opportunity to pay it forward and help others. In 2005, when I first started my own business, I met an older executive who owned an ink manufacturing company here in Charlotte. We were talking, and he opened up about how he could have sold his business for big money years back and been set for life—not only him but also his sons. However, he didn't sell, and since then, the market for ink had shrunk. It was disappearing.

He actually started crying during our meeting, and this was a tough-as-nails-exterior kind of guy. I got up, put my hand on his shoulder, and sat next to him. I said, "I'm sorry to hear this. Perhaps I can help you." He talked some more. I listened. I didn't sell him anything. That would have been taking advantage of this guy, who was down on his luck and, worse, guilt-ridden by the thought that he'd let down his sons.

Instead, I introduced him to two potential customers in the flexible packaging industry, hoping to help him increase his sales volume. The last time I spoke to him, he was not doing outstanding, but he was doing better. He had kept his business alive and felt like he had something to pass on to his sons. I felt some gratitude that I'd played a tiny part in improving his situation. I can't take credit for his hard work and per-severance, of course. But I felt like, in that situation, I'd done the right thing—which was *not* selling—and that maybe that had helped him.

Like I said, I remember my old GE boss with great gratitude. Maybe the ink manufacturer has some small spot in his memory for me. I'd like to think so. But if not, that's okay too. Because I still feel good about what I did that day. I approached that meeting with a clean heart and a however-I-can-help mindset. I didn't make a dime. And I don't regret a freaking thing.

However-I-Can-Help Creates Connection—and Success

I just gave you an example of "Karmic Selling" where I didn't sell squat. That's going to happen. If you approach the world with a clean heart and a however-I-can-help attitude, you're not going to close every deal and win every dollar. But guess what: even if you're always trying to sell ideas or products to people to win them over and get their business—you're *still* not going to close every deal and win every dollar. With a clean heart and a however-I-can-help mindset, you'll at least get that warm, fuzzy feeling, and, in my experience, you *will* see plenty of wins. Success will come.

The however-I-can-help mindset has led me to close seven-figure deals, time and again. Here's one example: I was meeting with an executive who was having some operational issues. After talking with him, I realized that I had a presentation with some information that could help him work through the bottlenecks. I told him, "Hey, man, let me send you this presentation. You don't need to hire us. You're shedding a lot of people right now, and it looks like you don't have the cash to spare. So, I'm not here to sell you anything. But I can share some info that might help you." I sent him a presentation and my thoughts on how to fix this issue himself. He took that info and executed on it. That was it. No deal. No sale. No money made. I had no skin in the game and nothing to gain when I shared that presentation with him.

But about six months later, the same executive called me and said, "Hey, Stan. I'm on the board of a different company, an aerospace company. They need your help. I'd like to introduce you to the CEO to discuss a potential project." Of course, I agreed and I got a

$2-million project out of it. That was him coming back and helping me after I'd helped him. Karma.

I had another meeting with a guy—I'll call him The Skeptic—who approached me pretty aggressively. He wasn't just playing defense with crossed arms. He was actively pushing me away, metaphorically speaking. He wouldn't even make eye contact with me. He was looking away, checking emails, and dismissing our entire discussion. At one point, he even took a call from someone else.

As usual, I was in however-I-can-help mode. I saw that I wasn't going to sell him a project, but I also saw an opportunity to help him: he'd just let go a COO and needed someone new. I happened to know some people. I told him, "I know some really good COO-caliber people that I can introduce you to. I'm not looking for any money; I'm not a recruiter. There's no hook attached to it." He was still skeptical at this point. I think that he didn't even believe I was going to follow up with him. But I sent him some names.

Did he end up hiring any of the people I connected him with? No. But he saw that I'd actively tried to help him, with no personal agenda. There was nothing in it for me. The next time I met him, his arms weren't crossed. In fact, I remember he called me "buddy." I think my jaw dropped, to be honest. He'd gone from being openly surly to downright friendly.

This was the perfect example of a guy who didn't believe I was for real. He didn't *want* to believe I was for real. But I showed him, through words and, more importantly, follow-up actions, that I wasn't full of crap. I really was ready to help him, with no pay-off for me. He ended up not only coming to me for help with a project later—he also introduced me to another CEO who I *also* ended up doing business with. A double win.

Beware, Not Everybody Wants Your Help

Ever since my car accident, however-I-can-help has been my mantra for success. I've built my entire business on it, and I've surrounded myself with other people who understand and share that ideology. In my consultancy, The Kormac Group, we have a firm rule: no assholes allowed.

That brings me to a hard fact: not everyone is nice. Not everybody wants to be helped. Not everybody is going to believe you're for real, even when you've shown them your authentic self and tried to genuinely help them.

It took me awhile to come to terms with this fact, and it wasn't easy. I had my moments of doubt as I shifted into the however-I-can-help mindset after my car crash. I started my own consultancy about seven months after the accident. It was an uphill journey. I was doing all this prep work before meeting prospects, going to one meeting after the next, taking notes, and following up—and constantly trying to help the person on the other side. It felt like a lot of work with little reward.

> *Not everybody is going to believe you're for real, even when you've shown them your authentic self and tried to genuinely help them.*

At one point, I sat back and said, "Why am I doing all of this? It's not working." And then I'd meet a guy like The Skeptic, and I'd think, "Crap, what am I doing trying to help a guy like this? Did I get this all wrong? This sucks! I'm working my tail off. Nothing is moving. Karma, where the heck are you?" I let myself doubt. I questioned my whole mindset.

But then the karma started trickling in. The however-I-can-help mindset I'd brought into early meetings with folks like The Skeptic started to reap rewards. The seeds I had planted in those early meetings started to sprout and bear fruit. And I realized, "Okay, maybe I'm not wrong. Maybe this idea of helping others isn't crazy."

At the same time, I was getting better at weeding out the people who just didn't want to be helped—the handful of defiant skeptics I'd *never* win over. And one of the keys to making Karmic Selling work for you is recognizing The Stubborn Skeptic *who doesn't want to be helped*. I've got plenty of those in my past too—I'd be lying if I told you the however-I-can-help mindset is some silver-bullet solution, some magic pixie dust you can sprinkle to make business go your way.

When you're meeting with a person, if they're a good person, you look to help them. In the whole sales process—the prep, the first meeting, the second meeting, the third meeting, all of which I'll get into later—you're getting to know people. You're seeking to *connect*. And, in that process, you're learning who's a good person at their core—and who isn't.

Not everybody values Karmic Selling. Not everybody values however-I-can-help. Not everybody *wants* to be helped. What I've realized over the years is, you can't help everybody. And you don't *want* to try to help someone who doesn't want to be helped.

Part of Karmic Selling means ferreting out the right people. You still bring pure intentions to every encounter. You still look to help everyone. But they may not receive it. And then you have to make the call and say, "Hey, God bless and good luck," and go on your way. There's no need to be resentful. You can just steer away from those folks.

The thing is, these are probably people you don't even *want* to be working with. Identifying them and cutting them out—and cutting your losses—is usually the best. That's how you'll build up a circle of business friends you actually want to work with. No assholes allowed.

How to Have a However-I-Can-Help Mindset and Mean It

Karmic Selling starts with the clean heart I talked about in chapter 1. You can implement that idea, and take it from theory to action, by embracing the however-I-can-help mindset. It's just about doing the right thing and trying to help people without agenda or objective—without a hook. And when you do that and genuinely mean it, you'll get ten times the good you put out into the universe.

Here is how I implement the however-I-can-help mindset practically:

- *Research how you can help them:* Before you meet a person, do your research and start thinking about ways you can help them. There are a lot of ways you can help someone. Give them advice. Give them a presentation or research that can solve their issue. If you can't give them advice, introduce them to an expert who can help. Or maybe you can introduce them to a potential customer or supplier—or, as I did with The Skeptic, maybe you can connect them with a new potential team member.

- *Listen to what they're telling you:* A lot of people aren't going to say "I need help with X or Y." But if you listen to them, you can recognize points where they might be able to use your help. Be present with the person. Listen to their words. Read their body language. Pick up on their sore spot—like I did with the hard-charging Boston CEO, who was struggling with his plant down in Virginia. That's probably where they need help.

- *Ask questions:* Sometimes, when you're researching how to help someone, you might draw a blank. If that happens, *ask* how you can help. I'll tell people straight-out, "I'm not sure how I can help you. I've been listening to you and thinking about the challenges that you've been talking about. I'm struggling with how I can help you. What can I do for you? What kind of expertise or information do you need? Maybe I know someone."

Now, if you bring that however-I-can-help mindset to business, you can thrive. But I'll let someone else prove my point: meet Mike Harris.

CASE STUDY

Mike Harris (Managing Director, Manufacturing Strategy, The Kormac Group)

I met Mike when we were both working at Honeywell. He was running a military repair and overhaul business, and I joined the company shortly after and ran the sister business, a commercial repair and overhaul business. Later, I ended up helping Mike through one of the most complex operations of his career.

It's tough to judge authenticity at your first meeting. Ultimately, it's time and experience that defines whether you're really getting somebody's authentic self. With Stan, I never had any doubts about that. At Honeywell, he supported me through a major overhaul, and I remember how he made it easy to drive big change because of his positivity and desire to do the right thing for his employees, his customers, and, quite frankly, me. He was a servant leader who played no games and was respected as a result.

Even after Stan and I moved on from Honeywell, we stayed in touch and helped each other with referrals, advice, and support. There was never any quid pro quo or judgment in our connection. The selfless way in which we helped each other built layers of trust that are still there today. The fact that Stan is such a master at follow-through helped: Stan doesn't just help, he follows up to ask, "Hey, was that useful? Is there something else I can do for you later?"

Fast-forward ten years and I found myself leading operations for a defense contractor. We were considering combining two divisions into one operating unit, which required some complex analysis. It was obvious to me that we needed a third party to drive the effort. Stan's firm was a clear choice. While my experience with Stan told me he was very capable of delivering a responsive analysis, my trust in him got him in the door. That trust was built over years of selfless interactions with an authentic person who truly seeks to help. That's Stan.

Help Others and Help Yourself

I've always had this attitude of wanting to help others, even as a kid. I was an altar boy from second grade all the way through my senior year of high school, and I remember my cousin, who was a nun, telling me, "Stan, you look so priestly." But I'm no priest. I'm also no saint. I had plenty of doubts as I shifted to the however-I-can-help mindset following my car accident. I knew I *wanted* to approach business— and life at large—with a focus on helping others. I'll be the first to admit, it wasn't always an easy road.

But I stuck with it. I noticed how helping others made me feel *good*. I noticed how helping others allowed me to develop relationships with awesome people and weed out the jerks. I noticed how those relationships translated into business success. Most importantly, I noticed how helping others allowed me to *connect* with individuals in meaningful ways.

I got hooked. I became addicted to that endorphin rush of helping others. That's what allows me to be so authentic in my however-I-can-help approach. I'm not looking to close a deal or make a sale. I'm genuinely looking for that warm, fuzzy feeling I get when I do something good and genuinely help someone. *That's* the pay-off. If my business benefits as well, great. If not, no problem. I've still connected with someone—and that feels awesome. The key to that connection? It takes more than simply wanting to help—it's about meeting people where they are. That's what I'll talk about in the next chapter.

REFLECTION EXERCISE
The However-I-Can-Help Challenge

Remember that warm, fuzzy feeling I've been going on about—that surge of happy endorphins you get when you pay someone a compliment or do something nice for them? I want you to experience that for yourself. Give that however-I-can-help mindset a try. It can be in your business or personal life. Try it out today. Then try it out tomorrow. And again, the day after that. Buy the person in line behind you a coffee. Compliment your wife, husband, or partner—thank me later. Hold the door open. Buy someone flowers. You might be surprised by the gratitude you get—and by how good it makes you feel. Make the however-I-can-help mindset part of who you are and notice how it comes back to you.

I'm obviously not the guy who invented 'random acts of kindness,' 'do unto others,' or even 'be kind—rewind.' People have been extolling the benefits of kindness forever. What I'm saying is that it's not just about how it helps others. It also helps you. You feel good—and, sometimes, you even end up selling something.

"Communication is merely an exchange of information, but connection is an exchange of humanity."

—SEAN STEPHENSON,
author of *Get Off Your "But"*

"A thousand fibers connect us with our fellow men; and among those fibers, as sympathetic threads, our actions run as causes, and they come back to us as effects."

—REV. HENRY MELVILL,
author and priest

C H A P T E R   3

The
Connection

People want connection. Now, more than ever. We've got so many barriers to connection: we're hiding behind our phone screens, we've got our ear buds in, we're Zooming instead of meeting in person. Our world right now is built to discourage connection.

But people still want connection—*authentic* connection. They don't want to be sold to. They want to feel like you're genuinely seeing them and hearing them, you're truly interested in them, and you really want to help them. And if you're going to help them, they need to trust you. The however-I-can-help mindset only works if you've earned a person's trust. That trust starts with a connection.

The good news? There are loads of ways to spark a connection. Compliment someone. Tell a joke. Make eye contact. SMILE. The first step toward a meaningful connection isn't going to be some grand gesture. It's going to be something small. It can be something as small as recognizing their name.

A name alone can open doors. I know this from experience. Very early in my career, I was the lowest level you could be at Goodyear. I was given the task of presenting a new kind of tire mold process to the CEO of Goodyear at the time, Stan Gault. We had been working on a prototype for a new kind of tire mold process at our little tire mold plant, and my boss gave me a clear goal: get Stan Gault, the CEO, the executive at the top, to give us the money we needed to adopt this new approach.

At this point in my career, I'd never even met a CEO. I had no clue how to talk to him. Stan and his entourage of hangers-on came to our little industrial plant in Stow, Ohio, in their nice suits and shiny shoes, and sat down in some rickety chairs in a back room. I was standing there, this young engineer in my workman's clothes, with my little prototype tire mold sitting on a beat-up metal table in front of me.

I was nervous. But I didn't show it. I started off with, "Hey Stan! Stan here. I really like your name." And it got a laugh out of him. It was a tiny thing—mentioning that we had the same name—but it woke him up. Then I went on to give my little presentation about the new process to make tire molds. At the time, it took us seventeen weeks to make a tire mold. With the new mold process, we could get it done in one week. We already had a patent for the thing. We just needed the money to scale up and implement it. I told him what we needed—I think it was half-a-million dollars, which probably translates to about a million in today's world.

We got it. Not only did we get the money; we also got our first order to start implementing that new mold process almost immediately. It was an order to fix up the tires on an older model of sedan. We barely had time to get the equipment and get those new tire molds up and running. But we managed. Goodyear got the bid from the automotive manufacturer, and I got a jacket out of it—a little nod to the part I played in helping us get that bid. I still have that jacket. And I still have a set of bookends modelled after that tire mold—patent number WO1998058786.

We had a great idea—a new tire mold process that saved loads of time. But that idea wouldn't have taken off if we hadn't secured the money that we needed first. Now, do I think that making that joke about Stan Gault's name was the key to getting that cash? Of course not. But it helped get the guy's attention. It had him sitting up in his seat and taking notice. It was the first step in making a tiny connection with him—one that ended in a positive business deal.

Connection Is Meeting People Where They Are

If you're going to connect with someone, you've got to meet them on their terms. Part of that means doing some prep work, including some research into the type of person they are (I lay out some steps for prep work in chapter 4). Meeting people where they are is all about adapting to their style in a way that makes them comfortable.

There's a psychological piece to this element, too. "Mirroring" is a known means of connecting with people. So, if you're talking to someone and they touch their face, you touch your face. If they lean back, you lean back. If they talk LOUD,

> *If you're going to connect with someone, you've got to meet them on their terms.*

you talk LOUD. If they talk *quietly*, you talk *quietly*. The concept of "mirror neurons" in the brain made a big splash in the early 2010s, and researchers have suggested that mirroring is a way to show empathy and establish connection with other people.[6]

---

6   Marco Iacoboni, "Imitation, Empathy, and Mirror Neurons," *Annual Review of Psychology* 60 (2009): 653–670, https://doi.org/10.1146/annurev.psych.60.110707.163604.

Don't overdo the mirroring—authenticity still matters! If you push it too far, your empathy starts to look like mockery. There's a lot more to meeting people where they are than copying their tone, gestures, or style. The key point is awareness: you've got to be aware of and sensitive to each individual's *way of being*. That is what takes an interaction with another person from communication to connection. In the words of author Sean Stephenson, "Communication is merely an exchange of information, but connection is an exchange of humanity."

An exchange of humanity requires awareness. That includes cultural awareness, situational awareness, and self-awareness—a knowledge of who *you* are as a person and staying true to that.

Cultural Awareness

I've worked with people across the United States and around the world, from Tokyo to Dubai. At a very basic level, when you're trying to figure out where to "meet" a person, start with culture.

My approach is tailored to the individual. If they're a hard-charger from NYC, there's no storytelling. They want bullet points. They want to know what the value is. They want to *get to the freaking point*. If they're a southerner, the meeting often starts a bit differently: "Hey, man, what's up? How's the family? Did you go deer hunting over the weekend? It's that season…" And so on. It depends on the person.

Of course, culture is just the starting point. People are all different, so you have to start by listening. They'll tell you who they are if you listen carefully, and then you'll know what approach to take.

I've had successful meetings that were fifteen minutes, right to the point, and sold the person—because that's what they wanted; they didn't want the small talk. I've had other meetings that lasted for an hour, where we talked for fifty-five minutes about personal stuff—from kids to cars—and then, in the last five minutes, it's "Hey, what about business?" Every situation is unique.

If you're working internationally, those cultural differences get even more significant. I spent some time working in Japan, and one thing I learned early on was the importance of the business card. When someone hands you their business card in Japan, you take it with two hands and bow to show respect.

Then, you can't just shove that business card into your pocket and say "thanks." You've got to take a moment to read it, acknowledge what it says, and acknowledge the person: "Oh, I see you're the CEO." You just make that simple comment—it shows respect. Those kinds of details matter because they can make or break a connection.

The importance of cultural awareness was also made clear to me in a business meeting I had in Dubai. The meeting was scheduled during Ramadan. I didn't know squat about Ramadan, but I did some research before I arrived and got the basics—so, I knew that Muslims would be fasting during the day, when the sun was up.

When I met with this gentleman in Dubai, I could tell right away that he was exhausted. The poor guy was practically falling asleep in front of me. I understood why; he hadn't eaten all day. Instead of trying to push through that, I met him where he needed to be met. I told him, "I know this is a busy time for you both personally and professionally. Maybe what makes sense is for us to meet again in two weeks. We can have a deeper discussion then." There were two weeks left in Ramadan at this point. I didn't mention that specifically, but he understood what I was saying—and he appreciated that sensitivity. He got alert right away and looked at me, and I could tell that he knew I'd connected the dots.

He ended up signing a deal on the spot. He said, "Stan, I know what you're saying, and I thank you for that. Normally at this phase, I'd negotiate to get your prices down. I'd look for a better deal. But what you proposed is fair, and I think your team can do a good job for us." He signed the agreement on that day.

I was floored. I'd barely told him about my company at that point; he'd just gotten a look at a first proposal. But I'd made a connection with him through that tiny bit of cultural awareness, and I think that's what sold him. That earned his trust and his confidence.

That cultural awareness translates in personal life, too. When I took my wife and daughters to Paris for a vacation, I made sure we all learned a few phrases of French beforehand: *bonjour, bonsoir, s'il vous plaît, merci beaucoup*—simple stuff like that. Now, was our pronunciation correct? Probably not. It was probably like nails on a chalkboard to the locals. But we were trying to meet everybody that we met respectfully, using their language in their country. People appreciated it.

At one point, we got lost, and I used my broken French to approach a stranger on the street and ask for directions. He helped us, without question. I gave him some money as a thank you afterward—we were really turned around and tired, and that situation could have ended badly without his assistance. But we made it back to our hotel without issue. We never had any problems the whole time we were there, and I think it was largely due to that little bit of extra effort on our part—just trying to meet people where they were by speaking their language, in this case literally.

Situational Awareness

Culture is just one part of the puzzle. You've also got to have awareness of a person's—or, in some cases, a company's—unique situation. How does that situation impact their needs? How does it influence your approach toward them? How does it change *where they need to be met?*

I've seen a lack of situational awareness torpedo a business deal more than once. I'll give you one example. I was in a business meeting with a potential client in the vehicle manufacturing industry. My consulting firm had already made it through a few rounds of meetings with these folks. So, now my team and I were sitting in front of the company's C-suite. One of the guys with me was still learning the ropes. I'd brought him along to observe more than anything.

The meeting was going well. My other teammate was giving the proposal, and the suits in the room were listening. The key decision makers were the CEO, a boisterous guy, and the CFO, a serious woman who was quietly sizing us up. So, we wrap up the presentation and we're in talks, and the CEO is talking and not letting anyone else get a word in edgewise. Hey, as the CEO, that's his prerogative—when he's got the mic, we let him talk.

But my new guy, the green guy, wasn't having it. He tried to interject a couple of times. Then, when he couldn't get a word in, he lost it. He got to his feet—and this was a big guy, so he was towering above the room when he stood—and he slammed his hand on the table and raised his voice.

He got everybody's attention. But he also scared the crap out of everyone at the table. I noticed immediately that the client executives recoiled. Despite the obvious shock and disgust at the table, our guy kept trying to get his point across.

I knew in that moment that we'd blown the whole thing. We'd lost their trust in that moment. Even worse, I later learned that one person at the table was in the middle of a contentious and abusive divorce. So, the last thing they wanted was to have a big, physically imposing person slamming things around and raising their voice.

We made the opposite of a connection in that meeting. It was a serious disconnect. I tried to salvage it and told the CEO and CFO later that we'd be happy to bring someone else in—they didn't have to work with this guy from my team. The CEO didn't mince words. He basically said, "If those are the caliber of people that you've got at your company, I'm not interested in working with you." And I don't blame him.

Self-awareness

That "what not to do" anecdote above shows an embarrassing lack of self-awareness. The guy who blew up in the meeting was not registering how his actions were impacting the other people in the room. All he was focused on was being heard—to the detriment of the other people present (and our potential deal).

You probably know people like that, too. They're so determined to be heard that they don't bother to listen. That's a bad approach for anyone, including the boss, but it's a *disaster* for a salesperson.

That brings me to the last point when it comes to connecting: you've got to be self-aware. In my world, that means being aware of who you are as a person and how your actions influence other people. Self-awareness means being true to yourself. It's the opposite of being the "sales guy" in the blue leisure suit. You're not putting on a mask. You're being true to you.

Self-awareness nurtures authenticity, and that's something people appreciate. Nobody wants to feel like they're being lied to, right? Nobody likes a fake, a fraud, or a phony. We want to foster real connections with real people.

> *Self-aware-ness nurtures authenticity—and that's something people appreciate.*

I think about this whenever I watch the movie *Tommy Boy*,[7] an old favorite of mine. Tommy, played by Chris Farley (RIP), is sitting with Richard (David Spade) at a diner and orders some chicken wings for lunch. The waitress tells him the kitchen is closed and that only cold dishes are

---

7   *Tommy Boy*, directed by Peter Segal (Broadway Pictures and Paramount Pictures, 1995). https://www.imdb.com/title/tt0114694/.

available until dinner. She's kind of rude about it. Tommy isn't fazed. He orders something else. No problem.

Then, he asks the waitress' name (Helen) and launches into this big monologue: "Helen, we're both in sales. And let me tell you why I suck as a salesperson." He goes on and on about how much he *sucks* at sales and how, every time he's close to making a deal, he blows it. The whole time, he's tearing apart this bread roll, representing his prospective "sale," in his hands, until he tears it in half—his ruined sale. Finally, Tommy tells the waitress, "That's when people like us have got to forge ahead, Helen."

Now, the waitress is looking at Tommy like he's freaking nuts. Richard, across the table from him, is looking at Tommy like he's nuts. Other people in the diner are turning around and looking at him like he's nuts. But Helen takes a beat, and then she tells him: "God, you're sick. I'll tell you what. I'll go turn the fryers back on and throw some wings on for you." Tommy gets the wings he wanted.

Afterward, Richard is staring at Tommy in amazement and asks him how he got the waitress to change her mind about the wings. Richard suggests that Tommy's ability to convince the waitress comes down to his ability to read people and to tell them what they want to hear. I see this scene a little differently. I think Tommy got what he wanted because he was true to himself: an unhinged, unfiltered, unpolished *non-sales* sales guy. His rawness resonated with the waitress. *That's* why she went and turned the fryer back on. That's why Tommy Boy got his wings.

How to Establish Meaningful Connections That Matter

Meaningful connections start with authenticity. You've got to be yourself. That's the most important thing. You've got to let out your inner Tommy Boy and be unapologetically *you*. That said, you can adapt the way you approach people while being true to you. By adjusting your approach to the individual, you're meeting them where they are.

Try these tips to meet people where they are and spark connections that bring results:

- *Do your research:* Try to glean insights into a person before you meet them. If you're meeting someone from another country, you might look up that country's business norms and general customs. My experiences in Dubai and Tokyo are great examples. Good research goes much more in-depth than that, though, considering a person's complete personal and professional profile. I'll talk more about the preparation that goes into the first meeting in the next chapter.

- *Read the room:* All the research in the world can't fully prepare you for the actual interaction. Observe a person's verbal and nonverbal language at all times. Keep an eye out for signs of those crossed arms, mental or physical, and adapt your approach as needed. If you see someone loosen up at the mention of their cat, talk about the freaking cat! Show interest in what interests them. Again: meet them where they are.

- *Be ready at all times:* This is something I'll talk about more in chapter 5, which is all about the first meeting, but it's worth a mention here—always be ready to connect. A "first meeting" can happen at any time. That woman sitting next to you on the plane? Maybe that's a future boss. The guy in the Uber with you? He could be a potential supplier. Always be ready to approach people authentically and strive to connect, whatever the circumstances. First impressions can happen anywhere.

Now, if you remain open and seek genuine connection with whoever is opposite you, whether that's a potential business friend or a personal contact, you can experience all kinds of wonderful rewards. I know because I've made rewarding connections in the most unexpected places—as you'll see from the case study below. Meet Kelly Short.

CASE STUDY

Kelly Short (Communications Director, Northern Forest Center)

I met Kelly at the Jacksonville airport. She was having trouble getting an Uber, and I offered to let her share mine. It turned out that Kelly had expertise in an area I needed help. I had no clue when I offered Kelly that ride, that my little act would benefit me in the way that it did.

I was at the Jacksonville airport, trying to get an Uber after a canceled flight—with no luck. I came across Stan and another traveler talking about rides, so I introduced myself and asked if there was any interest in sharing a ride. Stan was very gracious. He said he already had a car coming and invited me and this other gentleman to ride with him.

I sat in the back of the car with Stan, and we started chatting: "Who are you? Where are you from? What do you do?" When I said that I worked for the Northern Forest Center, Stan mentioned that he owned some forestland. I asked him what he was going to do with the land, and he said he wasn't sure. I told him, "There are resources for forest landowners who want to learn about their land or get advice about how to manage it."

So, I got dropped off—I offered to share the cost of the ride, which Stan refused: "Absolutely not." He gave me his card, and we parted ways. When I got home a couple of days later, I emailed Stan some resources and connections that I thought might be able to help him think about his options with his forestland. He ended up having a forester walk the land with him and talk to him about his priorities and how he might manage the forest.

It was a reciprocal moment all around: when he offered me a ride, Stan turned around what had otherwise been a very frustrating afternoon for me. And I was able to give something back that could be useful to him.

In a way, Stan's generosity in giving me that ride resulted in a much bigger benefit that goes well beyond me or him—it's benefitting the environment. Some people who don't know what to do with forest-land might clear-cut it for a quick payout. With the right resources, it's possible to build a long-term stewardship plan for the land that will take care of the water, wildlife, and other priorities—and keep the land producing trees for generations.

Connection Only Counts If It's Authentic to You

It has taken me hundreds, if not thousands, of instances of repetition to learn how to connect with people. Through trial and error, I've learned what works and what doesn't. In the end, it comes down to awareness—cultural, situational, and personal. If you approach the world with that sensitivity, you're on track for real connections. The connections you create *will* impact your life. Rev. Henry Melvill puts it more poetically than I ever could: "A thousand fibers connect us with our fellow men; and among those fibers, as sympathetic threads, our actions run as causes, and they come back to us as effects." Those effects can change your life.

But the most important point in all of this is that if you want to make real connections, you've got to be true to you. I'm not trying to create an army of Stan Gwizdak clones with this book. Every person is different. It's up to you to create your own approach and develop your own style when it comes to really connecting with people, but those above points will help.

Don't try to be someone else. Just be yourself. At the same time, strive to get to know the person across the table from you: their *authentic* self. The first step in really getting to know someone? It starts before you even meet them—it starts with the research you do before your first meeting. That's what I'll talk about next.

REFLECTION EXERCISE
Create a Connection

Make an effort to start connecting with the world in a more mean-ingful way. Look for small opportunities every day to connect. Try it with somebody in a cab, like I did with Kelly. Try it with whoever's cutting your hair. Try it at your favorite coffee shop. Your barista who makes your coffee every morning—do you know their name? If not, ask them. Practice creating a connection with people you meet and reading those verbal and nonverbal cues to figure out how to meet that person on their level. Reading those nonverbal cues also means being able to tell when it's not the right moment to connect. If the person next to you on the plane has their headphones on, they're obviously trying to have a moment for themselves—and that's not your moment to connect. However, you'll find plenty of other people out there who are surprisingly open to connection. Find them and practice. The more you do it, the easier it gets.

"One important key to success is self-confidence. An important key to self-confidence is preparation."

—**ARTHUR ASHE,** tennis champion

CHAPTER 4

The Prep

ere's a fun fact that usually gets me some crazy looks: for a one-hour meeting, I put in three hours of prep work. No, that's not a typo. Three hours is the amount of time I try to invest in researching a new client. Why?

The prep work is the most important part of building connections. Most people think it's the first meeting and the initial impression you make there. However, to make a good impression in that first meeting, you must be comfortable and confident. You have to know *how you can help them* and be able to articulate this in that first conversation. Preparation is the key.

Prep work can look a lot of different ways. One of my favorite tools is

> *The prep work is the most important part of building connections.*

LinkedIn, which I've been using for years. When I first started my consultancy in 2005, it was just me, myself, and I. Drumming up new clients as one person wasn't easy. LinkedIn was my go-to. Back then, when the platform was newer, you could connect with a CEO, and they'd actually reply to you.

I used LinkedIn to start conversations, and, in some cases, get new business. I was already using the Karmic Selling method at that point, so whenever I connected with a potential client, I'd emphasize connectivity. My opening statement was, "I prefer to be more than just an email address on the other side of this message. I looked at your profile and I see what you do, but please tell me more." At the same time, I'd be using their profile to research them and their company, so I could start a useful, informed discussion that really served that person.

This approach opened up conversations with folks all over the world, from the United Arab Emirates to Europe and beyond. I truly tried to help everyone I met, and it worked. I got business through LinkedIn, from a contract with a company in Dubai to a partnership with a Lean consultancy in Seattle. I landed business with a bunch of different companies, including General Dynamics, BAE Systems, ThyssenKrupp Elevator Systems, and others.

Today, LinkedIn is still a powerful tool, but the novelty has worn off. Honestly, so many folks use it the wrong way, it's almost turned into a spam platform. I get two to three LinkedIn sales pitches in my inbox every week: "Hi Stan, I'm sure you'd love to have more customers. Please get back to me and I can help you grow your business by 25 percent or more." I can tell from these pitches that the person hasn't taken any time to research me or my business. I just delete them—because I can see right away that the person hasn't bothered to do their prep work. That's not the kind of person I trust with my business.

Don't Show Up to a Meeting Naked

You wouldn't show up to a meeting without your pants on, except maybe in a very bad dream. To me, neglecting prep work is the same thing. When I haven't done the prep work, I go into the meeting feeling naked—meaning, I don't know how I can help the other person. It's easier to have a clean heart when you're prepared. My prep work helps me figure out both who the person is and where they need to be met—and how I may be able to help them. It helps me determine what I can bring to the table.

I don't mean that in terms of providing a service. Often, it's giving something away for free, like a useful professional connection or information. CEOs are used to people *asking* them for stuff. So, if you're the person sitting in front of the CEO and offering something for free, you're going to stand out. If you did the prep work and listened, you'll be able to offer something useful—and then you'll *really* stand out.

Prep work also builds confidence. Going into a first meeting, you've got to be confident. Prep work will give you the authority you need to ask smart questions, answer the other person's questions, dig deeper into their problems, and suggest possible solutions. That confidence often translates to success. As tennis champion Arthur Ashe says, "One important key to success is self-confidence. An important key to self-confidence is preparation."

Research has shown that confidence can be a driver for attraction in romantic relationships as well.[8] I think that confidence plays a similar role in the business world: people *want* to work with confident people. They're drawn to them. Perhaps they feel safer with them. I think this translates to business.

If you're not demonstrating confidence in a meeting, why should the other person have any confidence in you? Why should they place their trust in you? Confidence is key—and, for me, it starts with feeling prepared.

---

8   Sean Murphy, "The attractiveness of confidence," *The Society for Personality and Social Psychology*, September 16, 2015, https://spsp.org/news-center/character-context-blog/attractiveness-confidence.

Prep Work Includes Researching the Person, Not Just the Company

I recently met with the CEO of a company that my consultancy was trying to engage for a project. As usual, I put in my three hours. I did the dirt-under-your-fingernails research, like reading annual reports and financial statements (I'll go into more detail on all the different ways you can prepare later). But I also looked at the CEO as an individual, not just at their company.

While researching this CEO, I learned that they'd been recognized as one of the most-admired C-suite executives of the year. It was a unique commendation that reflected on them, not their company. I made note of that before our meeting.

When we met, I brought it up: "Hey, nice job on being named a most-admired CEO. That means you're doing something right. Congratulations to you." Now, this was a pretty dry person. They weren't particularly warm; they always maintained a professional attitude. But when I brought up that accolade, they started smiling ear to ear. I could tell, they were really proud of that achievement (as they should have been), and my acknowledgment of it made them feel good.

That was it. The exchange ended there, and the conversation moved on to the next step. But in that quick moment, I saw the CEO's arms become uncrossed. They opened up to me, and we had a productive conversation as a result—all because I'd dug up that little nugget in my prep work.

Researching a Person Means Researching the Professional and the Personal

Just because you're meeting someone in a professional context doesn't mean you should neglect who they are on a personal level. If you know what makes someone feel good—whether it's their kids or their hobby collecting vintage cars—and you can connect with them about *that*, you're also building a connection. That connection can translate to a professional relationship.

I remember I had a meeting with the COO of a hospital in the Northeast US. As usual, I did my three hours of prep work. While doing my research, I discovered an AM radio talk show about health-care topics that the COO had created. It seemed to be a passion project—something they did on their own time.

I listened to some recordings of it, which were still available online, and jotted down my notes. One thing jumped out: they flagged three things that they considered the most important topics in healthcare: "X, Y, and Z" (I can't remember what they were now—this was years back)! But I remember I wrote down those three points in my prep notes.

Later, when we met, I quoted the COO's own words back to them. I told them, "Yeah, what I've realized is that the three most important things in healthcare right now are X, Y, and Z, right?" Needless to say, they did a double take. Then they told me, "I say that all the time!" I came clean and told them, "To be honest with you, those aren't my words. Those are your words." They said, "What do you mean?" and I explained, "I heard you say that on your AM radio show."

The COO was floored. They couldn't believe, first, that I'd found their show. Second, they couldn't believe that I'd taken the time to listen to it. I told them, "That's the level of preparation I do coming into my meetings. If we work together, you'll get that same level of commitment on any project we do." I sold a project to that COO. That hour of prep work I devoted listening to their AM radio talk show was an hour well spent.

I've seen this approach—addressing the professional *and* personal—work for other people, too. The next case study is a great example. You'll see it from both sides: Jeff Lindow's and Curt Howell's.

CASE STUDY

Jeff Lindow (Managing Director, The Kormac Group) and Curt Howell (CEO, Versalift, a Time Manufacturing Company)

I first met Curt back in 2013. My colleague, Jeff, has likewise known him for years. Jeff played a big part in nurturing our organization's business relationship with Curt, keeping in contact with him until we could find a way to help him. Prep work played a big part.

In Jeff's words:

We had been in contact with Curt for years—but we never found an opportunity to work together. Then, in late 2017, Stan and I were doing business in Texas, and we agreed, "Let's go see Curt." We had our meeting, and the first thirty minutes were just BS-ing—we weren't talking anything business- or shop-related. But I believe this is what made that meeting a turning point in our overall relationship.

Listening to Curt, I realized we had a few personal things in common. He's into martial arts, which was also a big interest for me, first as a kid living in Japan (military family) and later as a young adult. We talked about the discipline needed to succeed in all areas of life, including raising kids. So, that shared bond of fatherhood and discipline was something we really connected on.

Stan and I did our prep work on the business side and had some thoughts for Curt on profitability, as well as revenue growth, which proved interesting to him. In total, that meeting was maybe an hour, and we walked away with an engagement letter signed that day. It looked like a very fast close, but it was really a result of building on years of communication and preparation, which helped create trust. If we had not built that trust relationship with Curt, he wouldn't have given us the opportunity and signed that day.

From Curt's point of view:

Jeff and Stan have a very consultative approach to sales. When they talk to you, it's more of a conversation about what's going on. When we started talking, I didn't have a project for them. But over the years, we kept communicating. Eventually, there was some stuff going on in my company where I thought they could be helpful. However, I'd known them for years before that point was reached.

The fact that we started working together came from staying in touch, which built trust and a connection over time. During one meeting, Jeff saw a picture in my office of me breaking bricks. It was from years ago, 1987, and I was doing a martial arts demonstration. Someone had sent me the photo along with a quote, "Never mistake gentle for weak." It was a fitting gift for me at the time, because back then I looked like this nerdy student, but there I was, breaking bricks in the evenings. Jeff commented on the photo, and it turned out that he'd done martial arts, too. It was just one of those weird things you don't expect—a random link.

So, I'd already gotten to know Jeff and Stan over the years, thanks to the continued communication, and by the time the right thing came up—a project I felt they could help me with—I was already pretty confident they were the right team. I could tell that they knew what they were talking about. When you're in an industry for decades, it's not that difficult to tell the difference between experience and BS, you know? By the time we worked together, it was obvious to me that they were going to be very effective—and they were.

How to Make the Most of Your Prep Work

You might be wondering how the heck you're going to fill three hours of time with prep work. Once you start, you'll find that those hours fly by. Try these steps the next time you're preparing for a meeting and see how long it takes you:

- *Look at their LinkedIn:* Check the person out on LinkedIn. Have they made any posts? Have they commented on any posts? Peek at their photo. Are they a buttoned-up person with a professional headshot, or is the image they present more laid-back? Try to read them. Make it a game and see how often you're right about the person based on their LinkedIn profile alone. Through LinkedIn, you can also check details like where they went to school, past jobs, and what they've shared. Search for commonalities.

- *Check their social media:* LinkedIn isn't the only social media platform worth scoping out. See if they have a Facebook, Instagram, Twitter, or other public social media account. This is a great way to get an idea of who you're meeting—which can help you determine how to *meet them where they are.* Are they married? Do they have kids? Do they love to travel? What hobbies do they have?

- *Read their company reports:* Read their annual reports and recent quarterly reports to get an idea of any current initiatives or ongoing issues they have. Think about how your company can fit into those initiatives, or address holes in their earnings or revenue.

- *Google them:* You never know what you might find about them or their company. You might discover that they have a podcast they host in their free time or that they've recently won an award. Google has it all. I also suggest specifically searching in Google News, which will highlight recent headlines and interviews.

- *Search for people you know in common:* See what common connections you may have with the person. If you have time, reach out to your shared connections and ask for insights into the person you're going to meet. Focus especially on connections within their industry. Also, make sure nobody in your company has met them before (and if they have, ask for details about the meeting and the individual).

- *Look for other commonalities:* It doesn't always have to be professional. Look for common points in your personal lives. Maybe you're both into martial arts—or you both have big families or both love to travel. Maybe you both collect miniature porcelain frog figurines. You never know.

- *Research their industry:* Read industry magazines to understand current activities and trends in their field. You can also reach out to people you know in their industry for insights into current issues. Find out what the pain point is. Where is the squeeze happening and how can you help address it?

- *Dig:* Dig, dig, and dig some more for information. Don't just scan the headlines that pop up on Google News. Actually *read* the stories. If you see that the person you're meeting gave a speech at an industry event, watch a YouTube video of it. If you see they have a podcast, listen to an episode.

- *Leverage AI:* Ask your favorite AI tool to summarize the background of your prospect, their company, and their industry. AI can add value at the end of your research process by checking your work and closing any gaps in your findings, but be sure to double check for accuracy. There's no substitute for investing your time and thinking through the information yourself given that your ultimate objective is a genuine, live connection with another person. AI alone can't prepare you for that.

If you've ticked off all those boxes on the list above and it's only taken you one or two hours, you're probably wondering what the heck to do with that third hour. Two things:

First, you need to use all that research to draft questions for the person. You're going to want to ask them about what's going well, where they're having problems, and what their needs may be. As you ask those questions, you'll pepper in things you've learned from your research. This will help create a more honest and productive conversation. I'll talk more about how to use your research in the following chapters.

Second, think about how you can help that person. Remember, your meeting prep is all about getting to know the individual who will be sitting across the table from you in the first meeting. That first meeting is when you want to go in with your clean heart and figure out, *how can I help this person?* Prep work will begin to shape that answer.

What If You Don't Have Time for Prep Work—or It Doesn't Work?

Sometimes, you won't have time for prep work. Three hours is a lot when you're swamped. Other times, you might not have time for prep work because that first meeting will happen in a place and at a time when you don't expect it. First meetings can happen anywhere, anytime, something I talk about more in chapter 5.

In other instances, you'll do your prep work and have a great conversation with the person, but you still won't know how to help them. If you come up with nothing, a great phrase to use is, "I feel helpless. I don't know how I can help you. I thought about it. I thought about it last night. I thought about it on the car ride over. I've been thinking about it during this entire meeting. But I still feel like I don't know how to help you. What are you looking for? What would be magic pixie dust that I could leave with you today?" Just ask them outright.

Point being: no amount of prep work can guarantee that you'll have all the answers 100 percent of the time. It's okay to say that you didn't have as much time to prepare for the meeting as you'd have liked, or that you did your research but came up empty-handed as to how to help the person. What's *not* okay is bullshitting the other person. It's like lying in a job interview: odds are, you'll be found out. Then you've lost that person's trust for good, and the first meeting is all about establishing trust. Millissa Flanagan knows this from years of experience—she'll share her perspective next.

CASE STUDY
Millissa Flanagan (Chief Operating Officer)

Before I met Millissa, I noticed that she had a background with General Electric, my former employer. Even though I was no longer with GE, I thought the connection was worth a mention—and it helped us build a rapport.

Stan's connection to GE and a recommendation by an operating partner within my network was the reason we connected. I was impressed in our first introductory meeting because I could tell Stan had taken the time needed to research my background and my business. As a result, he knew exactly what I was looking for, and portrayed the confidence needed to continue the conversation. It was because of this and his genuine approach that I felt that he understood my need and could meet it. That was the larger component for me: he took the time to get to know his audience, the company, and the pre-determined need.

For example, Stan knew my background was in integrated operations and advanced manufacturing. During our discussion, he immediately established common ground by using manufacturing language. Then, after that first conversation, he consistently followed up. He's not afraid to make a call or send a text and ask, "How can I help?" And if he can't help you meet that need, he'll find somebody who can. That also goes a long way in demonstrating trustworthiness.

Knowing your audience and how to connect with them is critical, and it's a piece that many people miss because they're too focused on preparing a pitch deck or practicing their presentation. If you know your audience, you're able to connect with them in a more genuine manner, "Well, what does this person actually want? What do they need? How can I help them be successful in that versus just landing this deal?" I could tell that Stan had taken the time to do exactly that.

Prep Work Plants the Seeds for Long-Term Relationships

There are lots of ways to prepare for a meeting. From listening to podcasts to checking a person's LinkedIn and researching them using AI, we've got more research options than ever before. In my career, the one thing that's remained constant is the amount of time I put into prep work: for every hour of meetings in front of someone, I plan for three hours of prep work. Even as information and research tools advance, this three-to-one strategy still seems to fit the bill.

My commitment to prep work has served me well. One consulting company I worked for, before I opened up my own shop, clearly revealed the importance of prep work. At that company, I had colleagues that never prepared for a meeting. They almost prided themselves on their ability to pitch on the fly. After one year, most of those guys were stuck in the same role, while I'd been promoted to a more senior role. I think the prep work I put into each client meeting is what made the difference.

I've seen prep work help other people, too. In the early days of LinkedIn, I gave seminars on using the site to advance your career. I knew a guy who had been let go from his corporate job and was looking for a new role, so I invited him to attend my seminar for free. He applied what he learned in that seminar and landed a new job within a month.

Now, it's great to see that kind of pay-off. A new job, a promotion, a raise—these are awesome things to have. But that's not why I'm so crazy about prep work. I like to prepare because it allows me to be more comfortable in my own skin. When I'm prepared, I'm more confident. I don't get that "naked" feeling in the meeting. I can approach it with that however-I-can-help mindset because I've done my research and, ideally, come up with some ways to help. If I haven't, I admit that freely.

Prep work isn't some magic pixie dust that guarantees you'll close a deal, but it can reap long-term rewards. In many cases, I didn't sell a project to a client immediately. However, I still planted seeds that led to a connection—as happened with that hospital COO when I told them I'd listened to their AM radio show. And then I watered the seeds over the years and harvested fruit, maybe three, five, or even ten-plus years later.

Prep work is the foundation for lasting connections that stand the test of time, including assembling a team of business friends you truly enjoy working with—something I'll talk about in chapter 10. I was reminded of this during the COVID-19 pandemic. During this time, a difficult period for most businesses, it was the relationships I had with old clients, seeds I'd planted as far back as 2010 in some cases, that helped my consultancy stay afloat. With much of the country on lockdown, almost nobody was taking new meetings, but those older relationships still bore fruit.

But before you can get to that point and reap the rewards of those long-term relationships, you've got to get through the first meeting. After all, that's what all your prep work is leading to. And that's what I'm going to talk about next. Chapter 5 will dive into the first meeting, how to think about it, and how to approach it when you are "live" with a customer in front of you.

REFLECTION EXERCISE
A Meeting Prep Checklist

Preparing for a first meeting and not sure where to start? Make sure you've checked these boxes. Have you...

- Connected with them on LinkedIn?

- Looked at any other public social media accounts?

- Read their company reports (financial statements, annual reports, etc.)?

- Put their name and their company name into Google and Google News?

- Checked if you have any shared connections?

- Searched for other commonalities (companies you've worked for, events you've attended, hobbies you have, etc.)?

- Researched their industry (read trade publications, talked to experts in the field, scoped out the latest headlines in their area)?

- Used your favorite AI tool to find out about industry hot buttons, areas of issue, and details on the person you are going to see? Hint: always check for accuracy.

- Drafted questions to ask the person based on your research? Hint: see chapter 7 for help on this point.

- Thought about how you can help them?

*"No one cares how much you know
until they know how much you care."*

—THEODORE ROOSEVELT,
26TH President of the United States

How to Kick Off the First Meeting (M1)

A fter prep work, the first meeting is the most important part of Karmic Selling. This is your chance to go in with a clean heart, demonstrate the however-I-can-help attitude, and establish a meaningful, lasting connection. To put it a lot more simply: the first meeting is where you show the other person that you *care*.

Like the Theodore Roosevelt quote at the top of this chapter says, "No one cares how much you know until they know how much you care." Prep work is showing someone you care. It's showing them that you've taken the time and energy to research them and their needs before the meeting. It's showing respect. It's showing a desire to help. Don't try to be the smartest person in the room. Try to be the most interested person in the room, who also happens to know a lot.

So, going into that first meeting, ideally, you'll have done your prep work. That's going to build credibility. You can show that you know what you're talking about. It's your chance to show the person sitting opposite you, "Hey, I care about you!" Simply demonstrating that you've taken the time to get to know the person and their issues makes a good first impression. In some cases, your prep work will reveal points of connection that can make that first impression even stronger.

The best example I have of this is the story of how I met Rich Holder, who I still talk to today—in fact, I've asked him to contribute to this book, and you'll read some words from him below. Rich and I met in a business context. As a senior executive, Rich had already seen plenty of consultants come in and out of his door. He knew to expect a pitch and to approach it with the appropriate skepticism—keep those arms crossed. As an executive, you've got to take this defensive stance, because people are always selling you.

So, I met with Rich, introduced myself and my company, and laid out a high-level agenda for the meeting. Somewhere in those introductions, I flagged the fact that Rich had worked at Eaton in the past—something I knew thanks to my prep work. I happened to know a person at Eaton, so I asked Rich, "Any chance you know George?" It was a shot in the dark but worth a try. What do you know, Rich replied that he considered George a great friend.

In that moment, I started to see Rich's arms come uncrossed. We had found a commonality—not only a person who connected us, but a person that Rich trusted. So, I told Rich, "Look, I'm paid to tell you that I'm great and my company's great. But why don't we call George and you can ask him what he thinks about me." I knew George's word would carry more weight than mine.

Rich agreed. I scrolled through my contacts and found George's number—and gave him a call on the spot. Luckily, he picked up. I told him, "Stan Gwizdak here. I have Rich Holder with me. He might be calling you soon himself to ask about me." Then I put George on speaker, and he told Rich, right away, "I'm not sure what you guys are talking about, but you can't go wrong with Stan on your team."

That was all it took. After ending the call with George, Rich and I chatted for a few more minutes. I could see that his attitude had shifted. He went from closed mind and closed arms, to immediately laying his issues on the table. He told me where he needed help and what I needed to do if I wanted to win his business and work with him. But I'll let Rich tell you about the experience himself.

CASE STUDY
Rich Holder (CEO, HZO Corporation)

When Rich Holder and I first met, we discovered a friend in common—George, someone Rich knew and trusted. That connection helped kick off a productive first meeting, which turned into a second and a third and…. Well, it's been over ten years and I now consider Rich not just a business contact but a true friend.

Stan and I first met around 2013. I had just taken over my first public company, and I was looking for someone to help get our operations in order. At the time, we had a group of basically rogue starships wandering the universe and sending money back to headquarters, and we needed to get that organized from an operations perspective. So, Stan was one of the many people I was meeting with at the time to make that happen.

One thing led to another, and George's name came up—and it turned out that Stan had worked with George. Now, I have great respect for George. We've worked together at two different companies—in fact, at one company, he was in my leadership tree and later, at another company, those roles were reversed, and George reported to me.

George taught me a lot about business. He's also the person who told me, "Hey, business gets done on the golf course" and taught me to play golf. Most importantly, I trust George. I know him to be a guy that runs a business in the same way that I personally want a business run. So, when Stan mentioned he'd worked with George, I figured, "Hey, if you can move in that circle legitimately, then you're at least worth listening to."

Stan's connection to George immediately brought credibility. When I was looking for someone to help get those rogue starships in line, I knew I needed someone with hands-on operations experience. Not everybody has that, even if they have a high-level title—and the last thing you want to do in that kind of scenario is to hitch your wagon to one of those people. For me, if you have a connection that can attest to some level of confidence and competency, you're halfway through the sale. And that's what happened when Stan mentioned George.

A First Meeting Isn't a Sales Meeting

I always tell my team that a first meeting, an M1, is not a sales call. It's about exchanging information that provides value to both sides of the conversation. We get to know a potential customer; meanwhile, we provide them with something of use, be it information, a connection, or some other kind of help. It's the first step in getting to know each other and making what I call a "business friend." In some cases, that "business friend" becomes a personal friend too—something I discuss in chapter 10.

I often tell people in that first meeting, "I see today as nothing more than an introduction to each other." This helps them uncross their arms, mentally and physically. It doesn't work for everybody: a hard-charger who wants to get to business might ask, "Then why are we here?!" As always, you've got to read the person and meet them where they are. Over the years, I've gotten better at that and learned to refine my approach—from my phrasing to my intonation—so I can better connect with the person across the table from me.

Regardless of who I'm talking to, I like to start off the first meeting with a quick introduction and provide a high-level agenda. I keep the introduction to myself and my company short and focus on them. This is a chance to show off some of that prep work. I might tell them, "I'd like to learn more about you and your company. However, I cheated and already did some research about you and your company..." And then I'll detail some of my prep work: "I checked out your LinkedIn," or "I read your most recent annual report."

If I found a point of connectivity with the person that I'm talking to in my prep work, I also highlight that here. "I saw you went to Penn State—hey, me too!" or "Hey, I also used to work for GE, do you know this person?" Those are just a few examples of how you can establish personal rapport through prep work. You might discover other possibilities during your conversation with them.

In my consultancy, we have a sort of guidebook for new employees that lays out tips for success, including how to prepare for a meeting and how to succeed in meetings one, two, three, and beyond. To give you an idea of how much importance I place on the M1, that handbook devotes twenty-four pages to M1—and just nine pages to the second meeting (M2) and third meeting (M3) *combined*. Interestingly enough, those twenty-four pages of guidance for M1 boil down to just three objectives: identify the other person's needs, set the M2 to continue the conversation, and build credibility. Below, I give some examples from my own career to show how those action points can be achieved.

Identify Their Needs—the Secret to Uncrossing the Arms

In chapter 2, I talked about the "crossed arms," literal and metaphorical, that you'll face in the business world. The first meeting is your first chance to uncross those arms. That's why it's so pivotal.

From my experience, one of the most effective ways to overcome the crossed arms is to embrace that however-I-can-help mindset—and that all starts with identifying the other person's needs. You've got to figure out where they need help, even if they don't want to admit it, and then do your best to give them some solutions.

Sometimes, you might see a need arise during your prep work. I previously mentioned a CEO I met in Boston—the hard-charger who used to work for McKinsey. He didn't want to tell me what he needed. When we first met, he was acting like his world was picture-perfect. But, because I'd done my prep work, I knew it wasn't. From his company's financial reports, I knew he had a plant down in Virginia that was having quality issues. So, I asked him about it, and he admitted that there *was* an issue.

I identified the need. Then, I offered him a (free) solution: I took a report I'd done for another company that addressed a similar issue—morale problems impacting quality—stripped out the identifying details, and shared it with him. That won him over. I think it's what got me the M2 and, in the end, a business project.

The case of "The Skeptic" I referred to in chapter 2 is another example. He didn't have a business need that my company could help him with. There was nothing we could sell him. However, during our conversation, he revealed that he needed a COO and I happened to personally know a few people who could fill that role for him, so I connected him to them. Again, the result was uncrossed arms. In fact, in the next meeting, he greeted me with "Hey, buddy." It was a Jekyll-and-Hyde moment.

My point is: sometimes the need will be obvious from the prep work; other times, you'll have to dig to find it. That's something I'll discuss more in chapter 7.

M1 Can Happen Anywhere, Anytime— Always End It by Setting Up M2

The second objective of your M1 is straightforward: you want to secure the second meeting, M2. This is especially important if you have a less traditional M1. I've met potential business contacts in all kinds of crazy places—elevators, airports, taxis, and planes are all spots where I've made connections.

I was sitting at an airport restaurant with a colleague of mine, Dave Antis, after a meeting. Dave had his nose in his laptop, as he was busy writing up a report based on our meeting notes. In fact, you'll hear from Dave in chapter 8, which is all about the importance of note-taking.

So, with no one to talk to, I was getting bored. I struck up a conversation with the guy next to me. What do you know, this guy worked for Nestlé. He was headed for Switzerland, but the US plant reported to him. He told me that they were struggling with some pro-ductivity issues and asked if that was the kind of thing my company handled. Yup. It sure was.

I made sure to set up a second call with him on the spot—and it wasn't even with me, because I wasn't in the food manufacturing branch of the consulting firm I was working for at the time. I set up the meeting for him and a colleague of mine who specialized in that area. Basically, I was the M1—and I sent the M2 to the right expert.

More recently, I had a similar experience at a Christmas-themed pop-up bar. I'm talking candy canes on the walls, inflatable snowmen, Santa statues—this place was Christmas on steroids. I was there with an old friend of mine, Marie Kelly, and I happened to strike up a conversation with someone at the bar. It turned out they had a business need I could fulfill. That led to a business deal. Now, we didn't strike a deal next to the inflatable Rudolph. But I made sure to set an M2 and we took it from there. You'll get the full story from Marie herself in chapter 7.

Whether you're in a conference room or at a Christmas-themed bar, the objective is the same: get that second meeting in the books before you leave the room. If you can't secure a second meeting, set a concrete date for a follow-up. It's as simple as saying, "Hey, I see there's nothing I can do for you right now. How about I follow up with you in X months and see where you're at?" Then make a note of that follow-up in your calendar—and stick to it.

Tried-and-True Tips for a Successful M1

I've been lucky enough to see more successes than failures in my career. Over time—and a lot of trial and error—I've come to recognize the steps that make for a successful M1. It looks something like this:

1. *Prep, prep, prep:* Have knowledge of the industry, company, and individual. All the while, think "How can I truly help this person?" Refer to that prep work as the conversation progresses.

2. *Establish a connection:* Use your prep work and background to develop a genuine connection.

3. *Build a rapport:* Whether it's a personal or a professional rapport, start sowing the seeds for a lasting relationship.

4. *Demonstrate credibility:* Build credibility for yourself and your company, proving that you are who you say you are.

5. *Set a non-sales agenda:* Set the agenda and clarify the structure of what's going to happen in the meeting, so they know what to expect.

6. *Identify areas of need:* Ask questions, probing for both current and future areas of need. Demonstrate your interest in them through a genuine, two-way conversation—something we'll discuss more in chapter 7.

7. *Develop an interest in their product or service:* Don't just get to know the company. Take a deep dive into their offering. Know their products and services as well as your own.

8. *Know the money matters:* Demonstrate awareness of the business financials, so you can anticipate the savings or growth they may expect from hiring you and your company.

9. *Confirm what you heard:* As they talk, make sure to listen, take notes, and circle back. If they mention a specific problem, come back to that. Dig deeper.

10. *Refer to your prep work:* If you sense that they're crossing their arms again, come back to the preparation you did. What were the initial needs you identified or points of connectivity you noticed? Revisit them.

11. *Remain helpful:* Maintain the however-I-can-help mindset. Remember, this meeting is not a closing. Find ways to offer value, from making personal connections to sharing relevant research.

12. *Remain watchful:* Observe their body language and tone. Look for signs that they're closing their minds or crossing their arms. When that happens, skip the sales talk.

13. *Be prepared for tests:* Anticipate questions like "What do you know about my company?" This is a test. It's your chance to show off your prep work.

14. *Set the M2:* Get the next meeting on the calendar before you leave. If you can't get them to commit to a meeting, commit to a follow-up date. You might say, "I see that I can't help you right now. When is a good time for me to follow up with you?"

M1 Isn't Where You Close Deals— It's Where You Earn Trust and Demonstrate Credibility

Preparation can help make your first meeting a success. But an M1 can happen anytime, anywhere, with anyone. Be prepared for that possibility. Either way, you have three primary aims: identify the other person's needs, set that M2, and build credibility. Remember, it's not a sales pitch. It's just two people getting to know each other and seeking to connect.

> *Remember, it's not a sales pitch. It's just two people getting to know each other and seeking to connect.*

When you approach the M1 with that however-I-can-help spirit, you'll find it pays off. I know because I've seen the numbers. When I was still working for other consulting firms, one of my managers approached me and said, "Hey Stan, congrats, you've got the best meeting conversions." I was still pretty green at the time, so my response was along the lines of, "Huh?"

Turns out, the big consulting firms track this data. For each salesperson, they check how many of their M1s convert to M2s; how many M2s convert to M3s; and, of course, how many of these meetings convert to sales. At the time, I had a 45 percent conversion ratio from M1s to M2s. The company average was hovering around 20–30 percent, so he said. Looking back, I think the approach I took to the M1 made all the difference. I hadn't yet developed the formal process of Karmic Selling, but I've always been someone who likes to get to know people and connect with them authentically. People felt that.

It's all in that first meeting. You either plant a seed that will lead to a great connection—a "business friend"—or the interaction dies on the spot. There are no guarantees, no matter how much you prepare. Still, I've found the greatest success with the however-I-can-help approach. Show them you care, and demonstrate your credibility. It's that simple.

Remember, you'll face skeptics. People will challenge you. They're suspicious that you want to help them; they assume you just want to sell them. So, they'll often test you. They'll float something in front of you, like an easy sale, waiting for you to jump on it. If you try to grab that sale, they'll sniff you out and dismiss you.

For example, they might ask if you can help them with an easy project, something their own in-house team could do. If you say, "Absolutely, and here's what it'll cost you," they'll recognize that you're just seeing dollar signs. If you say, "Hey, you know what, I bet you have a team that could handle that. But what I can do is give you some information about similar projects we've done in the past. You don't have to pay us anything. There's no hook." Then they might actually want to hire you for something more substantial.

It all comes back to that clean heart, which helps you earn trust. You'll win in the end once you've connected and established credibility. Bring that clean heart attitude to your first meeting and you're more likely to get a second or third meeting. I'll talk about how to make those subsequent meetings effective in the next chapter.

REFLECTION EXERCISE
Your M1 Checklist

This checklist can help you ensure the success of your own M1s. Adapt it to your needs and make it your own.

- *Are you talking to the right person?* Is the prospect the relevant decision-maker? If not, who is? How do you get in the room with that person?

- *Is there an area of focus?* Has your prep work and your first conversation revealed an area where they could use help? Are they willing to admit they need help? If not, can you dig deeper in the conversation and ask probing questions to get there?

- *Have you done your research?* Refer to chapter 4 and the reflection exercise. If you haven't done that prep work, you might not be ready for the M1. Remember, this includes research into the company *and* the individual.

- *Is the meeting framed correctly?* This is not a sales meeting! Set a clear agenda so that expectations are clear for both sides. Set up the idea of an M2 if necessary.

- *Have you mentioned common connections?* Who do you know in common? Have you mentioned them? Are they willing to act as a reference?

- *Have you provided case studies?* Where have you worked in this industry? Do you have case studies referencing similar companies or areas of improvement? Ideally, case studies will be for a similar industry and type of project/problem.

- *Have you dug deeper with questions?* The conversation is a two-way street. I talk more about asking and answering questions in chapter 7.

- *Have you wrapped up the meeting?* Always summarize the meeting, and follow up with a thank-you note. I talk more about this in chapter 8. The wrap-up includes your commitments and area of focus for the M2.

- *Have you established credibility?* Weave your prep work, background, and experience into the conversation to build confidence in your and your company's capabilities.

- *Have you set the M2?* Make sure to get it on the calendar before you leave. If you can't set a meeting, set a follow-up date.

- *What headwinds have you identified?* In the M1, you'll likely already get a sense of some hurdles that may interfere with a deal, like pricing concerns. Make note of those and prepare to address them in M2, M3, and beyond.

*"You can have everything in life
you want, if you will just help other
people get what they want."*

—**ZIG ZIGLAR,** author and salesman

CHAPTER 6

Tried and True Approach for Your Second and Third Meetings

(M2 and M3)

I f you've made it past the M1, you've already achieved something big: your potential client has given you permission to sell to them. Based on your M1, they have enough faith in your credibility and your capability to help them that they're willing to talk to you further.

I like to say that you've made a "business friend." Now, it's up to you to nurture that friendship through M2, M3, and beyond. That may mean going the extra mile—something I did quite literally in the case of Sarah Kirby, as you'll see.

Sarah and I met in a group phone conference around 2010. She was a VP of operations at a hospital that my consultancy was looking to work with. M1 went fine. M2 went fine. But then we got stuck. Sarah seemed ready to work with us, but she wasn't the only decision-maker in the room; there were a lot of other people involved—and a lot of objections to face down. Not everyone wanted to make the changes my consultancy was suggesting. For others, there were financial objections.

I saw that we had a big mountain to climb if we were going to work together. If Sarah was going to "sell" my consultancy internally, she'd have to overcome those objections. So, I suggested we work on it together. Sarah was in Columbia, South Carolina, and I was in North Carolina, just next door. I told her, "Why don't we do brunch on Sunday? I'll come to you." And she agreed.

So, that Sunday, I drove to meet her—literally going the extra miles—to discuss how we could overcome those internal objections. Together, we developed a strategy on how to approach them and meet our common goal of working together to improve the business. Guess what? It worked. My consultancy ended up selling the hospital a multi-million-dollar project.

But that one brunch wasn't just about signing a deal. That was over ten years ago, and Sarah is still someone I speak to today. She became and has remained a valuable business friend. I'll let Sarah tell you about the experience herself.

CASE STUDY

Sarah Kirby (former VP of Operations, Palmetto Health)

Sarah is a long-standing business friend of mine. I think our connection really took root when I offered to drive to South Carolina to meet her for Sunday brunch, so we could work through a shared business problem.

I've worked in operations for a long time and been approached by a lot of salespeople. As operations people, we're trained to face salespeople with our arms crossed. As executives, we'll even warn each other, "Hey, avoid hallway B, because there's a gathering of salespeople there." That's how on guard we are. The sales experience isn't always enjoyable.

When I met Stan, I was overseeing a large optimization project. Stan and his team were brought in to help with some process redesign to address efficiency, flow, and all that. So, as usual, when we first met, I had my arms crossed. But over our series of conversations, I opened up to him because I liked his non-sales style. He wasn't pushy. He was direct and a good communicator, but he took a helpful manner and tone when he talked.

That was solidified when we met for brunch that Sunday, for me especially because I'm a big believer in breaking bread with people I do business with. Working in hospital operations, my mantra when it comes to building teams has always been "Those who eat together, stay together." And I really commit to that theory in practice. I'm telling my teams, "Every quarter, we're going to do ice cream sundaes. We're going to do a baked potato bar. I'm going to work with the dietary staff to come up with something healthy for us to enjoy together. What do you all want to eat?!"

And that's worked wonders for our teams. Because when you're breaking bread with someone, you're not just talking about work. You're learning that, hey your kids go to the same school, or you go to the same gym, or the same church, or whatever it may be. You're discovering points of connection. From an operations standpoint, that helps to create teams that really work well together. So, I appreciated that Stan took that time to break bread with me. He made the sales experience that operations folks like myself usually shy away from an enjoyable one.

The Goal of M2 and Beyond: Keeping Your Business Friend

You can lose your business friend at any time—especially if you haven't known them for long. Even though your new friend has given you an opening to sell to them, you don't want to be seen as a salesperson. In the second meeting, they're still going to be wondering, "Is this person for real? Are they trying to scam me?" You've still got to keep an eye out for and overcome the crossed-arm mindset.

If you see someone's arms crossing, literally or metaphorically, the best thing you can do is take a step back from selling. Come back to your clean heart. Just like the M1, the M2 is not a sales meeting! You're still getting to know your client and their need to figure out how you can help. You might open with something like, "So, today's meeting is really all about us diving in deeper on what we discussed last time. You said you've got this particular issue. I've come prepared to talk about that. Is that still in the mix? Is that still something you're interested in diving into deeper?"

This may be where they'll step back and get worried that you're trying to sell them. So, tread lightly. Explain the steps: "Today, I don't have anything to sell you. I'm looking to help you. Today's conversation is about figuring out how to do that." In the course of the conversation that follows, you're also trying to quantify their need. Then, at the end of the second meeting, you try to get that third meeting, the M3. At that point, you're basically asking for permission to come back with a proposal on how you can help them. Securing your M3 is an ideal end to the second meeting.

> *Even though your new friend has given you an opening to sell to them, you don't want to be seen as a salesperson.*

The third meeting is very similar. Again, what you're looking to do is to have a deeper discussion on the potential client's particular pain point—which you've successfully identified in the M1 and M2. So, for the third meeting and beyond, you're digging deeper into that pain point while maintaining your connection. All the while, you're focusing on keeping your business friend.

Know That Things Won't Go According to Plan

Now, in an ideal world, you'll have your first meeting, where you'll make a connection and identify a business need. In the M2, you'll quantify that need and come up with ways to help address it. And then, in the M3, you'll come in with your proposal and closing. That's ideal. But very rarely is it actually M1, M2, M3, deal closed. Very rarely.

I've had client partners where the relationship started way back in 2010, and I didn't sell them a project until 2018 or later. That's okay.

I stayed with a clean heart, looked to help, and, in the end, we were successful in working together. But we sure didn't sign on the dotted line right after M3. Here's an example of that in action.

In 2012, I met an oil and gas services company. My consultancy was invited to take part in what was essentially a beauty pageant. We were competing alongside tons of other consultancies, including some much better-known names, to help with facility consolidations. So, we went in, presented our approach—and lost. A consultancy that had already done some work with the CEO in the past got the bid. Fine. No problem. The CEO went with a name they knew and trusted, which is understandable.

In 2016, my consultancy was invited back to the same company, this time to pitch the creation of a shared-services business model. After that pitch, I thought we had it. I was like, "Yes, we're finally in." Nope. We lost again, this time to a better-known firm. Now, this one really stung, because I'd stayed in their corporate offices for a full week, aligning with the CEO and the team on what a shared-services model could look like and how they could implement it, and giving them thoughts and advice on how to do it. I thought we'd won it.

When we didn't, I had a moment of doubt. I thought to myself, "Wait a minute, I stayed here on my dime for a freaking week, gave you all this free consulting, and we didn't get it?" I was a little bit jaded about my clean-heart approach at that point, as you can probably imagine.

Then, in 2018, we were invited to pitch *again*, this time for a project doing a total transformation of the company. And *again*, we lost to a much larger consulting company. At this point, I was ready to throw my hands up and say, "Forget it guys, I'm done."

But I stuck with it. I left the door open to future opportunities. And I'm glad I did. Because after about six months of the incumbent working on this particular project, we were asked to come in and look at some specific workstreams. We presented our approach to fixing those workstreams—and *this* time, we ended up signing a multi-million-dollar project.

Keep in mind, my M1 with this company was in 2012. The project we finally signed for kicked off in mid-2019. Again, in this process I always listened to the client, understood their needs, and met them where they were. In the end, a great partnership was formed, and four more projects followed with more on the horizon!

Look Out for Alligator Arms

You've made it past the M1 and are clicking along to M2, M3, and beyond. Things are looking good. But here's a hard fact: the closer your prospect gets to signing on the dotted line, the more hesitant they'll get. They will actively *look* for reasons not to hire you.

I call it "alligator arms." The closer someone gets to signing, the shorter their arms get: picture those little alligator arms, trying to hold a pen and sign a document. It doesn't work, right? I've seen it happen time and again: the closer we get to signing a deal, the shorter the potential client partner's arms get. They go into

> *The closer your prospect gets to signing on the dotted line, the more hesitant they'll get.*

alligator mode, with little itty-bitty arms that just can't... hold... the... pen... and... sign... the... paper!

Be ready for it. Don't let it rattle you. Understand it. They're going into very basic human protectionism mode. They're basically crossing their arms again and saying, "Why the heck would I hire you? Why *you?*" They might poke at you and ask some more tough questions, even though they've already asked 101 tough questions. Don't get offended. Don't lose patience. They're basically testing that little bit of trust you've built. The key is to remain in that however-I-can-help mindset.

My situation with Sarah is a great example. In that case, the objections weren't coming from Sarah directly—they were coming from other people in her organization. Whoever's objecting, you can't just sit back and hope for the best. You've got to face objections head-on and address them with facts and compassion.

If they're raising pricing concerns, give them a cost–benefit analysis. If they're worried about timelines, show them a case study you completed in a similar time frame. If they're stressing about credentials, give them a referral they can trust.

Entertain their doubt, but maintain your confidence. Be direct, and don't use wimpy words. When you address their objections, use positive language. Don't use phrases like "Well, I think," "Perhaps," or "Maybe." Say, "I understand your concern about pricing. Now, let me give you a cost–benefit analysis to address that."

And—here's where however-I-can-help comes into play—be prepared to go above and beyond. Like I did with Sarah, understand that you might have to go the extra mile. Take the weekend meeting if you need to. Odds are, you won't regret it.

Tried-and-True Tips for a Successful M2, M3, and Beyond

Just like the M1 approach in chapter 6, my approach to the M2 and M3 has evolved over the years through lots of repetition—and trial and error. I've tried a million different approaches and one thing I've noticed is that whenever I lost a client in the M2 or beyond, 99 percent of the time it was because I neglected to approach them with the appropriate authenticity and good intention. I didn't maintain my clean heart.

Every meeting you take after the M1 is your chance to prove that your however-I-can-help approach is for real. Show people you are who you say you are. Do what you say you will do. Look to help in any way you can. Expect that you're going to need to go back to rebuild your new business friendship at each step—make sure you stay in helper mode.

You'll find a more specific checklist for the M2 and M3 prep in this chapter's reflection exercise. As you put those concrete steps into action, keep in mind the tips below. They'll help you nurture and keep your business friend:

- *Prep, prep, prep:* Aim to be even *more* prepared when you go into the M2 and beyond. For example, for the M2, have relevant case studies and bios of the team members that will work with the client if they sign a deal. For the M3, have a draft confirmation letter ready to discuss and possibly sign.

- *Listen for and get ready to address objections:* Whether it's the M2, M3, or M112, be ready to respond to challenges. Be prepared to demonstrate how you've completed a similar type of project in the same space and have references ready. I always tell people, "Hey, I'm paid to tell you I'm great—but it's better for me to have somebody else tell you that instead." Then I give them a fitting reference to contact.

- *Don't oversell—but don't be a wimp:* Once you've gone beyond M1 and been given the implicit permission to sell someone, it's tempting to get more direct and to oversell. This is a surefire way to lose your business friend. Keep the discussion focused on *them* and their needs. While doing so, convey confidence.

Eliminate uncertain language—what I call wimpy words, like "well," "perhaps," "maybe," and so on.

- *Keep bringing value:* Instead of selling, focus on helping. Show up to every meeting with something tangible you can give the client for free. Maybe you read a relevant article or completed an applicable case study since you last saw them. Maybe you thought of another connection you can set them up with. Don't show up empty-handed.

- *Deliver on your promises:* Your business friend is still getting to know you. Earn their trust. One easy way to do that is to simply do what you say you're going to do. If you tell them you'll follow up on X date, do it. If you promise to send them a report, send it. If you told them you're going to find them a purple squirrel, you better darn well deliver a purple squirrel.

M2, M3, and Beyond: It's All About Keeping the Conversation Going

Whether you're going into the M2 or M500, your goal is the same: keep your business friend. Nurture that relationship. The way to do that? Remain ready to help. Like author Zig Ziglar says, "You can have everything in life you want, if you will just help other people get what they want." Identify the potential client's need and figure out how to meet it—and you're on track.

You want to approach your business friend with a clean heart. Leave them wanting more and realizing you are who you say you are. You'll still encounter skeptics. People who had their arms uncrossed may cross them again. Anticipate that and prepare for it. Most importantly, stick to your authentic path. Eventually, that business friend will sit back, uncross their arms, and say, "Well, crap. You're doing exactly what you said you were going to do. You haven't tried to steer me astray. You haven't tried to sell me a used Rolex. You're the real deal."

If you remain authentic, eventually people will realize that and let their guard down. It may take a while. And there will be some back and forth. As you go through those meetings after the M1, you'll still face tough questions and have to continue demonstrating your credibility. Chapter 7 talks about how to keep the conversation going in a way that will help you maintain your business friend.

REFLECTION EXERCISE
Your M2 and M3 Checklists

After an M2, ideally you'll have a scope of work identified; the client will have been qualified on their decision process and budget to proceed; and you will have given the client an idea of costs, timelines, and expected results. Still, expect pushback at this stage.

This M2 checklist can help you stay on track:

- *Have you introduced the meeting agenda?* Explain the objectives of the day's meeting and get their permission to move forward.

- *Have you reviewed the outcome of the M1?* This can include circling back to business *and* personal points. Remember the Jeep from chapter 1? I made sure to follow up and ask if it had been sold. Folks tend to forget us; we have to remind them of what was said.

- *Have you quantified the area(s) of improvement?* Has that goal been quantified, or do they need help measuring it? Will the project pay for itself and more?

- *Do you have references ready?* Have them ready to go but don't provide them until needed. You don't want to burn references on tire-kickers at this point.

- *Have you provided background information on your company?* This could be case studies, for example. They will help to answer the question of why should they buy from your company.

- *Have you provided value?* Stay in helper mode—for example, with the approach of "you *could* do this yourself—here's the formula." Give the client answers with value.

- *Have you explained your process?* Just as important, is the client clear on your approach—do they buy into it?

- *What is their decision-making process?* Who has the power to sign? Is it the person sitting across the table from you or is there an internal team you need to win over?

- *What headwinds have been identified?* Expect objections like "no money/time/resources," "the boss won't let me," "the Board says no," and so on. Keep these in mind as you prepare for the M3.

- *Is there a date for the M3?* Has the meeting converted? What commitments have you made?

- *Have you summarized the meeting?* Close the meeting by summarizing it, confirming next steps, and securing the M3 in the calendar before you leave.

For the M3, the objective is even simpler. The only thing you've got to ask yourself is: *Did you get the deal signed or not?* That's it. Ideally, you will have a signed deal; a start date; and a team defined on both your side and the client's side. However, as you can see from the examples above, many times the M3 doesn't go as planned.

This M3 checklist can help you stay on track:

- *Come prepared:* Have a draft confirmation letter written. I like to use the term "confirmation letter" instead of proposal. A confirmation letter simply confirms what's been discussed and agreed upon.

- *Expect push back:* You'll hear objections like the organization isn't ready or the money isn't there. Don't oversell at this point or you'll lose them.

- *Offer alternatives:* Don't push them to hire you. Give examples of problems like theirs and how those were solved. Give them the "out" or they may feel over-sold or trapped.

- *Listen:* Understand their concerns, and ask probing questions to dig deeper. Look for ways to find a solution without selling your services directly.

- *Stay in helper mode:* The M3 probably won't go as planned. Stay in helper mode and show them the way. Tell them, "You can do this without my company." Again, avoid overselling or cornering your business friend.

"Part of being successful is about asking questions and listening to the answers."

—**ANNE BURRELL**, chef and television personality

In Conversation

K eeping your business friend relies on constant conversation. That doesn't mean that conversation is always easy. You'll face tough, often skeptical, questions—especially the further along you get and the closer the client is to signing a deal.

I see questions as a good thing. Questions are a buying signal from the client. They're an indication of interest. They're a sign they are weighing the pros and cons. If the client doesn't have questions, it probably means you don't have a client. If the client isn't asking those tough questions, it means they've already written you off. They don't want to get to know you better. They're not interested in being your business friend. You don't mean squat to them.

> *Questions are a buying signal from the client. They're an indication of interest.*

If they *are* asking questions, they give a crap! That's something. Now, just like you can't expect an "ideal world" where you get the progression of M1, M2, M3, closed deal—you also can't expect to be prepared for every question you get. The key is being able to respond honestly and directly.

A great example is the time a client asked me to find them a purple squirrel. Okay, no, not a real purple squirrel. Let me explain.

I was meeting with a potential client partner, a president overseeing an entire division of a company. He was based in Europe and had a unique request: he needed a person who had some dirt under their fingernails and had worked an automotive assembly line floor—but who could also put on a suit and present to a board. This person had to understand how automotive assembly worked from an engineering standpoint well enough to hold their own when interacting with engineers from companies like Porsche, BMW, and Mercedes. They also had to have the kind of polished presentation skills needed to sell C-suite executives.

So, this president asked if I could find someone like that to design their assembly lines. I didn't hesitate: I told them, "Hey, have you ever seen a purple squirrel?" They said no. And I responded, "Well, you're asking me to find you a purple squirrel."

Which was true! They were asking me to find someone with a very high level of engineering expertise, who could go head-to-head with German engineers—and who could also stand in a boardroom and put on that blue leisure suit and sell a concept to the highest-level executives you could find. I truly didn't believe a person like that existed—a sentiment I expressed at the time.

But I said I'd try to find them. I told the president, "I doubt that person exists at the level you're looking for, but I will try to find them. I will try to find the purple squirrel."

Guess what? I found the freaking purple squirrel. But—and this is a big *but* for someone like me—that purple squirrel was kind of an asshole. Fair enough. He *knew* he was a purple squirrel. He *knew* he was one-of-a-kind. He was aware of that fact that he was, quite literally, one in a million.

But I'd made a promise. So, I presented the purple squirrel to the president who'd asked for it. I also gave the president my honest opinion of the purple squirrel—namely, that he would not be an easy person to work with. Finally, I told the president that I didn't think this role could be held by one person alone and that they would be much better served by splitting the role into two: one engineer, with some dirt under their fingernails, and one "salesperson" who could put on the blue leisure suit and present in front of the board in a way they'd understand and appreciate.

What happened? Well, the potential client partner ended up taking my advice. They met with the purple squirrel. They saw what I saw in the purple squirrel, and they decided not to hire the purple squirrel. They ended up splitting the role into two.

Finding that purple squirrel was no easy feat, and I didn't get any business out of it. Again, I'm not a head-hunter or a recruiter. When I connect people, I'm not getting any payout. Still, the president whom I'd found the purple squirrel for appreciated my help. While they couldn't offer me a deal immediately, they remembered the effort I'd gone to—and, a couple years later, they had a contract for me.

Why? They knew that if I promised something—even a purple squirrel—I'd deliver. That's why they chose to work with me. Because they knew that I approached business with a clean heart and a how-ever-I-can-help mindset: I identified the need and I tried to meet that need, even though it did not serve me immediately.

Prepare for Questions— and Prepare Your Questions

A conversation is all about getting to know the other person, whether in a personal or a professional context. You've got to answer the other person's questions *and* ask your own. It's a two-way conversation and an exploration of whether your business friendship is meant to be. Both of you are learning.

For you, it allows you to explore their needs and identify a goal— hopefully, it's a goal that you can help them achieve. By asking good questions, you can also enhance your credibility. You'll show that you know what you're talking about. This establishes a basis for trust.

Every client will have their own questions specific to their industry, person, and problem. Sometimes I get a question I could have never seen coming, like a request for a purple squirrel. Other times, I see the questions coming from a mile away and am ready for them.

Over the thousands of meetings I've held, there are some queries that come up again and again. At the same time, I've found that certain questions from my side can lead to a useful discussion. I've covered both sides in this chapter's reflection exercise. At the end of chapter 7, you'll find a list of questions to expect from their side and questions to prepare from your side.

But before we get to that, I want to cover some more general issues to anticipate when you get to the Q&A portion of the conversation with a potential client. First, be prepared to pivot at any time. Second, anticipate discomfort—and know how to deal with it.

Use Questions to Direct the Conversation

You can't prepare for every question you'll get asked. When surprise questions—like a request for a purple squirrel—arise, be prepared to embrace them. I didn't write off the request for a purple squirrel. I saw that it mattered to my potential client; therefore, it mattered to me.

If you're having trouble identifying a need through your initial questions, try a new approach. One favorite oddball question of mine is, "What's eating into your lunch hour right now?" I want to know what problem that person is facing that's got them chowing down at their desk (or skipping lunch altogether).

> *You can't prepare for every question you'll get asked.*

This happened recently with a business partner of mine—a senior executive at a glass company. He's a relatively new business friend. I hadn't really identified a need of his that I could address in our early conversations. So, I asked him, "Hey, what's got you working over lunch? What's got you staying late at the office? What's creeping into your weekends?"

When I phrased it that way, he knew the answer right away. He told me, "I've been having issues with the lids for my glass containers. I'm buying them all from China. The price is okay, but the tariffs are killing me. And the lids are okay, but they're not the best quality." This turned out to be a stroke of pure dumb luck, but *I actually knew a supplier.* I knew someone whose company specialized in container and lid manufacturing. So, I told my new business friend, "Hey, believe it or not, I know someone who might be able to help. Let me introduce you." I connected them on the spot.

The reaction I got from the glass company executive was one that drives home just why however-I-can-help matters. He said, "This is why I want to do business with you. You have always added value to me during our discussions." I'd managed to direct the conversation in a way that allowed me to meet my main objective: help someone.

Anticipate Uncomfortable Conversations

Like I said in the introduction to this chapter, I see questions as a good thing. They're an expression of interest. The person on the other side of the negotiating table is actually entertaining the idea of hiring you, giving you a deal, or whatever it is that's on the table. At the same time, the closer that person gets to signing on the dotted line, the more hesitant they'll get. You'll see those alligator arms I mentioned in chapter 6 come out.

At this point, you'll want to circle back to your prep work. This will allow you to come back to the need you've identified—and to reiterate how you can meet it. Based on your prep work, you'll also know what questions to ask to help draw out that need. You might have to get the other person to *admit* the need, which can lead to uncomfortable situations.

Take the Boston hard-charger I mentioned in chapter 2—the one who insisted to me that everything was fine with his business, but who was actually having problems with a particular plant in Virginia, something I'd found in my prep work. When he expressed doubt that we could help him, I came back to the research I'd done before our meeting. I asked about that plant. When he told me that it was a morale issue, I had a case study in my back pocket to show him, so I could say, "Hey, we've dealt with morale issues at manufacturing plants for a similar type of client. Let me show you what we did for them."

Now, did this guy *like* having this problem revealed, after he'd just told me that everything was good with his business? Nope. We had an uncomfortable few minutes there. I had called him out on something that he was basically trying to conceal. I was shining the interrogation spotlight on him.

When you do this, the other person will get uncomfortable—so you've got to tread lightly. You can't accuse them or give any kind of idea like, "Hey, you're a failure because this isn't working in your company," or anything like that. You've got to keep a sense of compassion and respect. And the way to do that is usually by asking questions.

Don't just say, "Well, I saw this plant of yours is underperforming." Say, "I saw this plant of yours isn't meeting the same benchmarks as the others. Can you tell me about that?" Ask the probing questions. Ask out of a place of genuine curiosity and kindness. Remember, even if you think you know the answers to the questions—even if you've done all your research and have some insider insights into what's going on—you don't know the company as well as the person on the other side of the table does.

That's how it worked with the Boston hard-charger and his Virginia plant. Only after I asked questions could he admit, "Yeah, we haven't gotten that Virginia plant figured out yet." That opened the conversation. Was it uncomfortable for a few minutes? Absolutely! But it did lead us to a fruitful discussion.

The same was true for the owner of the ink manufacturing plant in Charlotte whom I mentioned in chapter 2—the guy who cried in a meeting because he was so worried about his company's future. It was during the Q&A part of our meeting that he broke down. I was asking him questions, probing, trying to find his pain point. Suffice to say, I hit it. Was it uncomfortable? Yep. But it was the point that got us where we needed to be—finding a solution to help him and his business.

How to Have Business Conversations That Matter

The reflection exercise for this chapter includes a template of sample questions to expect and questions worth asking as you seek to connect with your new business friend. Here are some broader points to keep in mind as you approach that Q&A part of the conversation:

- *Make it a two-way street:* You aren't just answering questions. You're also asking them. You have the right to probe deeper. You're exploring potential areas of need from their perspective and trying to figure out where your business may fit. They know you're probing for that, which is okay. There's no need to apologize for it. Both sides are learning and listening. Prepare thoughtful questions. When you ask good questions, it establishes credibility on your side. It shows that you know what you're talking about.

- *Prepare for the skeptics:* When facing a potential client partner's question, you have to really know the product or service you're selling. That's step one. Because you can then recognize whether what you have to offer can meet their needs. That could mean having some case studies or technical specifications on hand. Sleep with them under your pillow. Absorb them. That way, when a potential client asks, "Hey, can you help me with this?" you can confidently say, "You know what? We can. Because we've already helped someone else with something similar." Quick, honest answers need to be part of your quiver.

- *Anticipate surprises and don't fake it:* There's often going to be a surprise question that you don't have the answer to. When that question comes up, don't bluff. If you have to, say, "I can't give you an answer to that right now but will follow up with an answer after this meeting." And then *do that*. If you don't know the answer, don't try to fake it, because you will lose credibility. You're better off being humble and staying truthful. At the same time, don't use wimpy words. Speak with confidence.

- *Treat their concerns with respect:* Some of the questions a potential client asks may sound trivial to *you*, but they matter to your new business friend. Therefore, they should also matter to you. Treat the client's concerns with respect and empathy. Remember that they are taking a risk with you.

- *Prioritize building trust:* Treat every conversation as an opportunity to build trust. This is especially important when you're asking probing questions that might make the other person uncomfortable. Be prepared to tread lightly, and give it the respect it deserves. Always come back to your core purpose: maintaining a however-I-can-help mindset.

Keep in mind that business conversations can happen anywhere, and they may not even start out as business conversations. My friend Marie Kelly has seen me transition a personal chat to a business discussion. I'll let her tell you about it.

CASE STUDY

Marie Kelly (Clinical Staff Pharmacist, UPMC Hillman Cancer Center, Pittsburgh, PA)

Marie and I have known each other since third grade. It's a friendship I cherish after all these years, and I try to see her whenever I'm in her neck of the woods. As mentioned in chapter 5, we recently met up for a holiday drink at a bar—where I ended up connecting with someone who turned out to be a business lead.

I'm a healthcare professional, so Stan's world is pretty foreign to me. I'm also more of an extroverted introvert, whereas Stan is very much an extrovert. We're different. But our friendship goes way back and, whenever he's in Pittsburgh—where I live now—we try to connect. This past December, we visited this pop-up Christmas bar, and I saw his idea of Karmic Selling in action and got a sense of how it worked.

We showed up to this bar and it was decorated like crazy. I mean, it looked like somebody threw up Christmas inside. There was tinsel everywhere and all these 1970s-style decorations: plastic three-dimensional Santa faces, ugly Christmas sweaters, and over-the-top ornaments and stockings hanging everywhere. All the drinks had Christmas themes and were served in some type of kitschy old glassware. It was a crazy scene. On top of that, the place was packed.

Even as we were waiting in line to get in, I noticed Stan engaging with everyone around us. And I was just kind of laughing to myself, thinking, "Man, he'll talk to anybody." Once we were inside and had our drinks, Stan struck up a conversation with a woman, and we all started talking. She was there with her husband, her daughter, and her daughter's boyfriend, and we ended up joining their table.

We were just laughing and having a good time, and then at some point, we made more formal introductions. And it turned out that the woman's husband was in a business that could use Stan's consulting expertise. So, before I knew it, they were exchanging business cards and setting up a meeting for the following week—right there, on the spot, in the middle of that Christmas bar. I would not have ever expected anyone making a business connection in that environment. But there you go. Stan did.

Real Conversations Build Trust and Create Connections

Real conversations aren't always easy to have. Like I said, they can be uncomfortable. They can even end in tears. That's okay. It's those genuine exchanges with another person that create connections and build trust. And it all starts with answering—and asking—questions.

For it to really make a difference, you've got to be listening with your however-I-can-help hat on the whole time. Chef Anne Burrell, whom I've quoted at the start of this chapter, gets it right: "Part of being successful is about asking questions and listening to the answers." Many people lack the ability or the will to truly listen, take in an answer, respond appropriately, and then probe accordingly. If you can master that skill, you've got a lot of the competition beat.

Asking and answering questions—and really listening—helps you maintain your stance in Karmic Selling. You're looking to help them through this dialogue. Sometimes the way to help them won't be obvious. That's why it's also important to realize that no detail is too small. Take notes about everything, both the personal and the professional. Listen for those little things that might seem inconsequential to you—while realizing they may mean a lot to the other person.

That's how you find ways to help. Conversing, listening, paying attention to the details—and making note of them. And that's what I'll talk about in the next chapter: the importance of taking notes and how to take notes that matter.

REFLECTION EXERCISE
Questions to Expect and to Ask

Keeping the conversation going is all about asking and answering questions. Be ready for both sides. This checklist of questions to ask and questions to answer can help. Flesh it out for yourself according to your industry, position, and goals.

Here are some questions you might ask in the M2, M3, and beyond:

- *What's your current market share?*

- *What's your organizational structure?*

- *What are your current _____costs?*

- *What current initiatives are you driving from your seat in the company?*

- *May I ask what's driving that?*

- *What have you done to fix it?*

- *How big of a problem is it?*

- *Are you happy with the progress and timing of the effort?*

- *Have you read/seen [research item]?*

Here are some questions to anticipate in the M2, M3, and beyond, and how to approach them:

- *What's your company's specialty?* Beware: they want to put you in a box. If you go too narrow, they might write you off for not offering the right *kind* of expertise. If you go too broad, they might write you off as a useless generalist. Now, you can't be everything to everybody. But odds are, if you've gotten this far, you can serve a need of theirs. I often say, "The work that we do is varied and I wanted to give an impression of the breadth and depth of our experience and what we've done for our client partners. Often, our initial scope will be small. But then our clients realize that we deliver—we do what we say we're going to do—and then our scope expands both in size and/or into other areas of business."

- *Why should we hire your company to help us?* This is where your prep work comes into play. Make sure you know what makes *your* company right for the job. Be prepared for tough follow-ups like, "Why should I choose your company over the competition?" Get ready to underscore what sets you apart.

- *Where have you done this type of work?* Anticipate follow-up questions, asking about details like your approach and the outcome. This is the biggest question I get in my field. Sometimes, I don't have an exact answer, usually because their problem is so specific. In that case, I might say something like, "That's a great question. I can think of a time where we tackled that. But, before I answer, can I ask some more questions to really understand what the issues are?" Then, after I ask my questions, I'll come back and say, "Okay, here is how we would approach that one." Make sure you understand their need.

- *How would you tackle fixing X problem?* This is one of those "surprise" questions you can't really anticipate. That empty bucket, the X, can be a million different things. If you've done your prep work, you'll have a case study you can pull out of your pocket and say, "Yeah, we've fixed that kind of problem for another company in the past. Here's how." Even better, you may have a referenceable client you can mention.

- *What are your typical fees?* Be prepared for objections to the pricing like, "I don't have the budget for that." Have a detailed cost buildup ready. As you talk, avoid wimpy words and stay focused on the benefits and return on investment. Make it clear why nickel-and-diming could hurt the outcome.

- *Do you have references?* Ideally, you'll have a common connection they know who can serve as a reference. I always like to say, "Hey, I'm paid to tell you how great we are. But our mutual connection, X, who I see you're connected with on LinkedIn, can tell you better than I can. We've worked with them and their company. Why don't you call them and ask them how we did?"

"Acquiring the habit of notetaking is therefore a wonderfully complementary skill to that of listening."

—**RICHARD BRANSON,** business magnate and commercial astronaut

CHAPTER 8

Noted

When I meet someone, whether it's in a boardroom or a bar, I take notes—about their business, personal details, and hobbies … if it matters to that person, it matters to me. Even if something seems small, I take note. Often small things are clues to bigger ideas. Business leaders in particular are unlikely to publicize their problems, but they might drop a small clue about a problem, which, for someone in my position, can open the door to a big area of opportunity.

Back when business cards were the norm, I'd jot down my first notes about a person on the card they gave me. This was especially useful at events like trade shows where you're meeting a lot of people in one day. I'd meet someone, get their card, and talk to them. Then, after I left their booth, I'd flip the card over and write bullet points on the back. If I felt like I had a connection with that person, I'd add a star to their card. Once I got back to the office, I'd scan the cards and digitize the information.

I had an experience at an energy industry trade show in 2007 that demonstrates the value of this approach. I was the CEO of a solar panel manufacturing company at the time, but I also owned a management consulting business, so I was there in a dual capacity. I met a person from a solar panel machinery manufacturing business who was having some problems with his company. I jotted down some notes: "wife, three kids, from Colorado, liked to ski" and some pertinent business issues.

I sent him a thank you after the trade show, and we discussed his business problem, but he didn't have an immediate need. He told me, "Yes, I foresee a need, but it's more like a six-months-out kind of thing." I followed up with him six months later (more to come on follow-ups in chapter 9). He never responded. No harm, no foul—I'm sure this guy met dozens of people at every event he went to, and he'd probably forgotten who I was.

I went to the same trade show the next year, and there was the same guy. I recognized him right away. Before I walked up to him, I checked my notes about him and his company, which I had in my phone, and refreshed my memory: *wife, three kids, Colorado, skiing.* I approached him and said, "Hey, how are you doing? Nice to see you…" We chatted for a bit before I told him, "Hey, you may not remember me, but we met last year." Then I brought up some of the personal details I'd just looked up—"I remember you telling me about the powder in Colorado," or "You mentioned you and your wife were looking to take a vacation"—whatever it was.

That's when this guy started really paying attention; he was basically like, "Wait, who are you again?" So, I refreshed his memory: "I'm the CEO of a solar panel manufacturing company, and I also own a management consulting business. Actually, you had a concern last year about getting some additional throughput in some of your manufacturing areas and asked me to follow up with you in six months. I did, but I know you've got a lot of stuff going on. I'm sure it got buried in your emails. Is that still an issue?" He said, "As a matter of fact, it is. It's an even bigger issue now than it was last year." We met for dinner after the trade show to talk about it, and I ended up doing business with him. A business relationship took hold—all thanks to the notes I'd jotted down on the back of the guy's business card at the trade show a year earlier.

Taking Notes Helps You Remember and Connect with Others

This book is really all about creating connections. Notes play a role in that because they help you remember the important stuff about a person. There's plenty of research around this. For example, studies have shown that writing things down on paper sparks brain activity—even more than when writing on a tablet or smartphone—potentially optimizing memory.[9] When you take a note, you're giving your brain a chance to process and absorb the information. And what you don't remember … well, that's what the notes are for!

> *When you take a note, you're giving your brain a chance to process and absorb the information.*

When I first started taking notes, I just scribbled down stuff on a sheet of paper. It was chicken scratch—hard to read and follow. I also tended to write too much, like I was trying to record everything the other person said verbatim. Nobody needs *that* much info in their notes. You're never going to read them if they're too long. So, over the years, I've developed some processes that help me take good notes.

---

9   Keita Umejima, Takuya Ibaraki, Takahiro Yamazaki, and Kuniyoshi L. Saka, "Paper Notebooks vs. Mobile Devices: Brain Activation Differences During Memory Retrieval," *Frontiers in Behavioral Neuroscience* 15, (2021): 634158, https://doi.org/10.3389/fnbeh.2021.634158.

Have a System for Taking and Organizing Your Notes

First off, pick your note-taking weapon of choice. I mentioned how I used to write notes on the back of business cards. That was a while back. Today, I use an electronic note-taking tool that I can write on with a specialized pen. It then syncs with the cloud and uploads my notes, so I can access them anywhere. Within the first twenty-four hours after my meeting, I have my notes transcribed. Then, I put those notes into my customer relationship management (CRM) tool.

Second, I recommend having a template that covers all three P's: preparation, professional, and personal. I worked for three consulting firms in between owning my own. All three used meeting notes. None included personal notes. I've created my own notes template, and it includes sections for both the professional and personal—you can find it at the end of this chapter. On the professional side, I might take notes about revenue, profitability, and market share—things like that. The personal side depends largely on the individual. I've jotted down notes about a Jeep. I've also jotted down notes about a person's skiing hobby, their pet dog, or the fact that they like to practice martial arts. I will jot down whatever seems to animate the person. I'm not looking to record their biography. Rather, I look for conversation openers to use in the future.

My notes template also includes a section for prep work. I split the page in half: on the left side is my prep work, so I've got that right in front of me during the meeting, and on the right side is where I add my meeting notes. You're welcome to take the template included at this chapter's conclusion and adapt it for your own needs, but you may find that you prefer a different note-taking method entirely. That's okay. The key is to find something that works for you.

Record Your Notes in a CRM Tool

You probably already use a CRM tool of some sort. If you don't, I highly recommend it. It lets you go back and easily search for a client by their name or company to quickly get all the information you need about them. You can see "Hey, we talked about these problems for their business," or "Okay, this is my ninth meeting with them," or "We met at that energy conference last year, I can reference that and ask if they're going again this year." A CRM makes it easy to refresh your memory quickly before a client meeting.

I like to get my notes solidified into a CRM within twenty-four hours after the meeting. As soon as I get my notes transcribed, I pop that digitized info into my system. If needed, I can add some color with additional notes manually. I do that while the meeting is still fresh in my head.

Once I finalize my notes, I take one last action to ensure I follow through on my commitments. If there's a follow-up date set, I make sure to add that to my calendar, with a link back to the client's profile in my CRM. Alternatively, if this is a person whom I feel like I can't help or connect with, I simply write NFN: no follow-up needed.

This book is all about connections and part of that means knowing who to *not* connect with—recognizing who isn't going to be a business friend and who you don't want as part of your circle of trusted friends. For me and my business, The Kormac Group, I've got to keep that "No Assholes Allowed" policy in mind. If someone isn't a good person, I'm not doing business with them, regardless of the possible revenue attached.

How to Make Note-Taking Work for You

I've evolved my note-taking over the years. Remember, at the beginning, I was scribbling everything down practically verbatim— my notes were hard to read and too extensive to be of any use. Over time, I've refined my technique. From that, here are some pointers that I hope can help you with your own note-taking:

- *Have your prep work at hand:* Like I said, I like to have prep information on the left-hand side of my notes sheet while using the right-hand side to take notes during the discussion. That way, I've got all the details on a single page.

- *Address professional points:* This could include company details such as facility details, revenue, EBITDA, inventory, and supply chain issues. Here's an example of what my professional notes might look like:

  □ *Leadership team is all new except for the ops leader (in place for two years).*

  □ *New plant in Alabama starting up in six months.*

  □ *On-time delivery needs improvement. $20 million spent on quality delays and issues.*

- *Don't forget the personal:* Take notes on the non-business details, too. This could include their partner's and kids' names, pets, where they're from, where they went to school, what hobbies they're into, and more.

- *Find a system that works for you:* I've described what works well for me. I've even given you my note-taking template at the end of this chapter. But you've got to figure out what works for you.

- *Use a CRM:* Make sure your notes are organized. Putting your notes into an electronic CRM also gives you a chance to review them (ideally within twenty-four hours after the meeting) and add some color.

- *Use abbreviations, bullets, and stars:* Summarize what you hear. Don't take it down verbatim. Use abbreviations. For example, instead of "revenue," I just write "R." Bullet points are helpful for capturing main points, while stars can emphasize key details.

- *Pay attention to the person:* Summarizing instead of writing verbatim is critical, because you want to pay attention to the person and maintain eye contact. While taking notes, you've still got to strive for connection. Check back with them: Are their arms closed? Don't just stare at your notepad or tablet. If I make a genuine connection and feel they are a good person, I write GP on my notes. GP means good person. This helps me focus on people I want in my circle.

Finally, you always want to review your notes as soon as possible afterward, so you can flesh out any details while the meeting is still fresh in your memory. That could mean consolidating and reviewing notes in a car, on a plane, or even at an airline club.

CASE STUDY

Dave Antis Jr. (Author and Operations Management Consultant, Antis Media)

Like me, Dave knows how important it is to capture meeting notes—and to get those notes organized ASAP after a meeting. On one occasion when we were working together, he took care of our note-taking, while I was able to connect with a new business friend. As I mentioned in chapter 5, it all went down at the airport restaurant.

Stan and I had a meeting with a potential client in St. Louis and were flying back out that same day. We were at the airport, sitting at this restaurant to get some food. I was busy reviewing our meeting notes and writing up a report—we always had to complete a report on every sales meeting we did together. So, my focus was on my laptop. I tuned out everyone around me, and I just had my head in my laptop.

Stan, being the relationship kind of guy he is, ended up chatting with the guy sitting next to him. It turned out that this guy was an executive for Nestlé; he was pretty high up and had several geographies under him for manufacturing operations. Before I knew it, Stan and this guy had exchanged business cards and contact information. Then, it turned out that the guy was on our flight, and Stan continued the conversation throughout the flight.

By the time we landed, Stan was on friendly terms with this guy and some trust had been built. Stan and I weren't in food manufacturing—we were in the widget manufacturing sector—but Stan still connected this Nestlé executive with the relevant food manufacturing expert at our company. Basically, he made the M1 happen at that airport restaurant. It was a good lesson for me, because I tend to get so focused on the task at hand—in this case, preparing that report—that I sometimes forget to take time and look at what's going on around me.

Notes Help Build Your Circle of Business Friends

Think of your best buddy. You can probably tell me a thing or two about them, whether it's their favorite sports team or how they spend their Friday nights. You've got mental notes about that person because you care about them. They're your buddy. When it comes to meeting new business friends, you can't name all that info off the top of your head. You've got to fill in those gaps. And that's where note-taking helps.

By taking accurate notes, you can build a picture of a person and their business, so you can get to know them and their challenges. This is what will allow you to eventually, if not right away, identify a need—a way you can help them. Then you can exercise that however-I-can-help approach and give them a hand.

Entrepreneur Richard Branson's quote at the beginning of this chapter says it well. When you are taking notes and summarizing the conversation, you're forced to listen to the individual—to *really* pay attention to what they're saying. You tune into the conversation and develop a deeper relationship as a result. You can then come back to those notes to solidify your relationship through appropriate follow-up that's relevant to the person's unique needs.

My notes at that energy conference in 2007 allowed me to appropriately follow up with the solar panel manufacturing equipment guy and return to a problem he'd mentioned almost an entire year earlier. Without those notes, I probably wouldn't have remembered that this guy had a wife and three kids and loved to ski, and I wouldn't have been able to reignite the connection in a meaningful way. Detailed notes, both personal and professional, are always handy in the follow-up—which is what we'll get into in chapter 9.

Meeting Prep Checklist

This meeting prep checklist can help you with your own note-taking.

 Download the PDF at KarmicSelling.com and adapt it as needed for your purposes.

Karmic Selling Meeting Notes Guide

Name: _____ Company: _____ Date: _____

MEETING PREPARATION	MEETING NOTES
Personal Research *Schools, places lived, activities, interests, spouse, kids, sports, nonprofit involvement, groups, etc.*	**Personal Insights** • • •
Company Research Performance Indicators *Current Year / Prior Year* *Revenue, EBITDA, ROE, cash flow, etc.*	**Issues Discussed** • • •
Acquisitions	
Divestures	**Need Help Areas** • • •
Initiatives • • •	
Notable Finds	**Follow Ups** Next Meeting Date & Time *Video Call or In Person*
Areas to Dig	Commitments Made *Information to send; introductions to make*
Who to Introduce	
Who We Know in Common	Agenda for Next Meeting •
Relevant Work/Prior Experience	• •

"Not following up with your prospects is the same as filling up your bathtub without first putting the stopper in the drain."

—MICHELLE MOORE,
author of *Selling Simplified*

CHAPTER 9

The
Follow-Up

S o, the meetings are all "over." You've done your research to prepare for each meeting. You've addressed and asked relevant questions. You've kept the conversation going. You've taken your notes. Now, it's time for the follow-up. This piece is just as important as anything else. Give it the attention it deserves—which means doing more than sending a cursory email after that last meeting.

I've already talked about how you can't expect the Karmic Selling process to go according to plan. It probably won't look like M1-M2-M3, and *boom*, deal closed. You may have five, ten, or even twenty meetings with a person before you find a way to help them. That's why reliable, regular follow-up is so critical. You've made your business friend. If they're a friend worth keeping, you've got to keep nurturing that relationship. Water the seed of friendship. Help it grow.

My business relationship with Curt Howell, whom you heard from in chapter 4, is a great example of this. Curt and I met in

2013, but we didn't find a way to work together until 2017. Then, after a single meeting in 2017, we closed a deal—in fact, we signed the paperwork on Friday and began work the following Monday. Someone from the outside looking in might say, "Wow, you guys are lucky! A one-day sale is a complete unicorn in the consulting space." Exactly: it doesn't work that way, and that's not what happened with Curt. The truth is that we'd been in consistent communication for almost five years before we signed a deal.

This example shows why follow-up is so important. You want to stay relevant and continue to meet your potential business friend where they need to be met. We had eight meetings with Curt before we found a way to help him. And, in the course of those eight meetings, we earned his trust. So, when a need *did* arise, he knew he could count on us. As a result, we won his business.

By the end of any meeting, whether it's M1 or M21, you will ideally have a follow-up date in your calendar and that of your new business friend. At the end of the meeting, take a beat and say, "When makes sense for a follow-up? Let's get it on the calendar." Set the meeting while you're still sitting across from them or on the Zoom line with them or whatever the case may be.

Author Michelle Moore sums it up perfectly: "Not following up with a prospect is the same as filling up your bathtub without putting in a stopper in the drain." Now, I prefer to use the term "business friend" over Michelle Moore's "prospect," but she's right that neglecting follow-up wastes opportunities because it's all about building the relationship that's been established. Every relationship is made up of the positive actions we do for each other, and every follow-up is a chance to take a positive action to strengthen that relationship.

Following Up Doesn't Mean Selling—or Begging

I've talked a lot about practicing authenticity and demonstrating reliability. Be who you say you are. Do what you say you're going to do. If you make a promise, keep it. By delivering on your words with actions, you're demonstrating that you're consistent and reliable, and you're building trust. Timely and relevant follow-up is the perfect example.

If you say, "I'll follow up with you May 15," then follow up with that individual on May 15. You can help build that trust even further by keeping your however-I-can-help mindset in place. You're never selling in your follow-up. Don't become a salesperson now! You've got to continue to think, "How can I help this person?" Add value so the client sees you as a partner, not a vendor. Maybe you read an article about their industry that you think could be useful to them or met someone in their field who could be a value-add connection for them. Whatever it is, try to find a way to help with every interaction.

You're never selling in your follow-up... Add value so the client sees you as a partner, not a vendor.

Now, you don't want to pester people, which is why you're also giving them permission to say no—something I'll talk about in more detail below. And you definitely don't want to beg them for business. It's not a good look and generally a turn-off for your new business friend. Below, I explain how to walk the fine line of being persistent without pestering.

Differentiate Between the Hard and Soft Follow-Ups

I put follow-ups into two buckets. The hard follow-up is about something concrete you've agreed to—say, working together on a project or selling a product. That one's straightforward. I might send an email that reads something like, "Hi John, Stan Gwizdak here. You said you wanted to sign this confirmation letter so we could get started on Monday. Where are we at? Did you have any questions or feedback for me?" There is a clear objective of the other person signing the confirmation letter.

The soft follow-up doesn't have a concrete objective. I might use it if the client was supposed to get back to me by a certain date, and that date has come and gone—and I still haven't heard from them. This type of follow-up asks nothing about the deal at hand. It's more about letting them know we're still there. I might write something like, "Hi Jane, I thought of you today when my team and I were talking about [a project that's relevant to that person]. We realized that the biggest gap we've seen in this kind of project is X." Then I provide some useful information on that point.

Alternatively, I might send them something like, "You mentioned you're having trouble with supply chain issues. We just did a similar project at another company. Here are some thoughts on how you can fix that." Then I'll include a relevant presentation. Or, I might just send along an industry article and say, "Hey, I saw this and thought it might be of interest to you." In the soft follow-up, you aren't mentioning a confirmation letter, contract, or deal. You're just reminding them, "Hey, we're still out here!" while also giving them something with tangible value.

Give Them Permission to Say No

This point applies especially to the hard follow-up: give them an out. Give them permission to say no. I used this technique recently on a client who had ghosted me. I said something like, "I'm just following up to see where we stand on the confirmation letter we shared. We agreed to a start date of May 1, but understand you had to push this project out for the time being. I'm okay if this project is dead." You can see how I'm giving my business friend permission to tell me *no*.

This way, nobody's time gets wasted—not theirs and, just as importantly, not yours. If I sense someone is stepping back, I'll ask outright: "This looks dead to me. That's okay. We can move on. Here are some ideas to drive this initiative yourself." You don't want to apply pressure to get the other person to close the deal. A low-pressure approach is something that people find refreshing and appreciate—which means that even if they aren't going to do business with you right *now*, they might be open to doing business with you down the line. Or, if they can't use your help, they might connect you to someone *else* who can.

I know this for a fact because it's happened to me. In chapter 6, I mentioned an oil and gas services company where my consulting firm, The Kormac Group, was invited to bid on a project in 2012. We bid and lost. We bid on another project for the same company in 2016, another one in 2017, and yet *another* one in 2018. None of them worked out. Finally, in 2019, we signed a multi-million-dollar project with them. I think it was largely thanks to the consistent follow-up and stick-to-it-ness we'd shown, coupled with our low-pressure approach. We always gave them permission to say "no," a right they exercised a few times before finally giving that big "yes."

The CEO of the oil and gas services company even said something about our low-pressure approach when recommending us to someone that reported to him. I've saved the introductory email he sent, in which he made the connection between me and a president in his company, because it's a reminder that Karmic Selling works. The oil and gas services CEO wrote, "I have found [Stan] to be a good industry connection and his low-pressure approach is refreshing." That really stood out to me; I remember writing a heartfelt thank-you email for that introduction, because I felt like it was a testament to how I try to approach business—with a clean heart.

Especially in a cut-throat field like consulting, a "low-pressure approach" is rare. But it works—and not just for me but also for other people. I'll let Kevin Nelson explain how it worked for him.

CASE STUDY
Kevin Nelson (Senior Executive, Medical Device Company)

Kevin is someone I consider not only a business contact, but also a friend. I met him in a consulting capacity and recall him remarking on my "non-sales guy"-like approach. Kevin himself is someone who's seen the merits of emphasizing authenticity in business dealings.

When I first met Stan, I was struck by his consulting firm's approach. He didn't push but connected very genuinely and made it clear that he and his team were all about solving problems. Between our first and second meetings, we had a few more touch points via email and phone, always with some practical, useful details. It never felt like a sales pitch. It was more about highlighting the problem and making suggestions to fix it. That really resonated with me.

Fast-forward about a year-and-a-half later, and COVID hit. I was asked to come in and talk to some of our customers—large hospitals— about the supply chain disruptions impacting healthcare. So, I took a page out of Stan's book and went in with the idea of having a conversation and asking, "Hey, what are you struggling with today? What's the problem? How can we help?" And they'd say (for example), "We desperately need syringes."

Some people might have sugarcoated the situation, but I chose to use Stan's approach and have an honest conversation about the problem. We talked openly about supply chain disruptions that were beyond our control: "You know what? We're still struggling to solve these issues. We can't sell you a solution that doesn't exist. But we can be transparent and tell you about the different angles and avenues we're exploring."

They really received that approach, just as I had, and what was at first a sort of hostile environment defused. We started that meeting at nine in the morning and the attitude was basically, "We don't want to work with you." By five in the afternoon, they were more relaxed and open to discussion. And they ended up sticking with us and even bringing us new business. In fact, I just had my 118th meeting with healthcare customers using this same approach.

How to Perfect the Low-Pressure Follow-Up

The follow-up, like every other step of the Karmic Selling process, is simply about nurturing a business friendship. You aren't begging for business. You aren't cramming a sale down someone's throat. You're looking for ways to help, while reminding them, "Hey! Remember me?" without applying the pressure.

Here's how I make it work for me:

- *Set the terms of the follow-up beforehand:* Ask your business friend when you should follow up with them. Let them set the terms, but get that date in both of your calendars before the current meeting ends. Then, follow up when they asked you to.

- *Follow through on the follow-up:* Once the follow-up is set, stick to it. If you have a meeting at 7 a.m., show up to that meeting at 6:55 a.m. If you're supposed to send an email on July 18, 2028, send an email on July 18, 2028. Deliver on your promises.

- *Understand the type of follow-up:* Is it a hard or soft follow-up? Tailor your messaging accordingly and consider giving them permission to say *no*.

- *Review your notes and be specific:* Reviewing notes from prior meetings can help with the follow-up. For example, you might address things you didn't originally respond to in the meeting. Be specific in your follow-up, not generic. Your notes will help.

- *Remain helpful:* Share an idea on how to help your business friend. You can send them a pitch deck, industry article, or connection. This is especially good for soft follow-ups.

- *Try different contact channels:* I like to mix up my follow-up formats. I usually start with a handwritten thank you. After that, I use all kinds of contact points. If they normally go through email, for example, send them a text or contact them on LinkedIn.

- *Give them permission to say no:* You want to be persistent. You don't want to be a pest. It still surprises me how hard it is for some executives to say no. Make it easy for them, and you'll make life easier for yourself.

- *Be genuine:* Whatever format you use in your follow-up, maintain your authenticity. Remember, by genuinely looking to help people, you'll ultimately end up helping yourself. That's what Karmic Selling is all about.

Remain Persistent to Start Building Your Circle

I've had people remark on my persistence more than once. My colleagues often note that I stay in contact with people and prospects for years, far longer than the usual sales cycle for my industry. Again, I really value that kind of feedback, because it lets me know that what I'm doing is working. In the past, I had moments when I questioned if Karmic Selling was effective. Feedback like that tells me that it works.

Following up is a key part of the process. It's your chance to stay relevant and continue to demonstrate authenticity and caring. Remember, you're looking to build a relationship, not make an immediate sale. Still, that however-I-can-help attitude may be met with skepticism. Some people will take the follow-up as a sales pitch, even when it isn't. They may reply defensively.

That raises another important point: follow-up creates a two-way street of accountability. Let's say you set a follow-up meeting, a date and time you've both agreed on, with a new business friend—and they ghost you. Yes, it happens. It's happened to me. At that point, you're well within your rights to ping them and say: "Hey, we set a meeting. You didn't show. What's up?"

A big part of Karmic Selling is simply about being authentic—do what you say you're going to do. However, that's a reciprocal arrangement. When you make a business friend, it's just as important that they do what *they* say they're going to. So, if they tell you, "Hey, I'll touch base with you about that deal by November 12," then they should touch base with you about that deal by November 12. This is how you'll be able to also start building your trust in them. It's how you'll be able to tell, "Hey, do I want to work with this person? Do I want them as a business friend? Do I want them in my circle?" People sometimes screw up, so don't expect perfection. But take note if someone consistently lets you down.

Because ultimately Karmic Selling is about building your circle of trusted friends—people who will value your authenticity, clean heart, and well-intentioned however-I-can-help mindset. Those are the people you want to work with. Chapter 10 talks about how Karmic Selling helps you find those individuals.

REFLECTION EXERCISE
Follow Up with a Lost Connection

Go back to someone you lost touch with—it could be a previous sale you didn't win or a client who ghosted you or a long-lost buddy. Follow up with them: "Hey, how's it going, I thought of you recently when I read X, and I realized it's been a while since we've spoken." You can also follow up from a personal angle: "I was planning a trip to France, and I remembered you'd been there, and I realized it's been a while since we've spoken. How are things?" Once you've got that professional or personal hook, take it a step further: "I've been wanting to reconnect with you. How's your schedule looking? When can we chat?" Give that follow-up a try and see what happens. The results may surprise you.

"Find your tribe. You know, the ones who make you feel the most you. The ones that lift you up and help you remember who you really are. The ones that remind you that a blip in the road is just that, a blip. They're the ones that, when you walk out of a room, they make you feel like a better person than when you walked in. They are the ones that, even if you don't see them face to face as often as you'd like, you see them heart to heart. You know that kind of tribe? Who's your tribe?"

—JENNIFER PASTILOFF,
author of *On Being Human*

CHAPTER 10

Growing Your Circle

I t took a near-death car accident for me to finally get that f— you chip off my shoulder. Cliché as it sounds, an experience like that really drives home the fact that life is short. You don't want to waste it being an asshole or dealing with assholes. You don't want to spend your days pretending to be someone you aren't. I've found that I'm the happiest and perform my best when I approach the world with a clean heart and surround myself with people who do the same.

Now, I'm not some freaking saint. I also get good out of helping others: when I help someone out, I genuinely feel awesome—I get a real rush of endorphins. It's almost like a drug. Once you start helping people out and realize how great it feels, you want to do it more and more. There will also be moments where people recognize your desire to help and that feels great too. In chapter 9, I mentioned the email I saved from the CEO who wrote that he found my low-pressure approach "refreshing." Similarly, I have another email saved, where a CEO from a company in Columbus, Ohio, whom I consider a great business friend wrote, "Stan, you always look to add value in our

KARMIC SELLING

conversations." That also felt great, because this person recognized my desire to add value—to help.

My Karmic Selling approach has helped me win business on many occasions, but, more importantly, it has also helped me earn valuable business friends, many of whom have become close personal friends. It has allowed me to build up a circle of people who I trust and can call on if I'm ever in need—and who I would happily help if they are ever in need. Author Jennifer Pastiloff's quote at the top of this chapter uses the term "tribe." I prefer the term circle because it speaks to a karmic aspect: you put out good into the world, and you receive good in return. The end result is a circle of awesome people to surround yourself with.

> *Karmic Selling has allowed me to build up a circle of people who I trust and can call on if I'm ever in need—and who I would happily help if they are in need.*

I'm always building my circle. Not that long ago, I was seated next to a woman on a flight from Pittsburgh to Charlotte. I could tell she was stressed out. We started talking. She worked in an industry I know nothing about, and it turned out she was stressed because she'd just had a job that did not go as planned. Long story short, her team showed up to the wrong location to do the job, while her client was waiting at the correct job site, wondering where the heck they were. These things happen. But this woman was really stressed about it. She told me, "I hope this client doesn't hold this against me."

Well, it turns out that the client was an old friend of mine. So, I pulled out my phone, opened Facebook, and sent my pal a message, explaining the situation to her—and ending with, "She seems like a really

148

great lady. I hope you'll give her another chance for me." My friend agreed. That's all it took—one small message on my part—and it turned around this woman's day. I also offered to introduce her son to a company in Baltimore, gave her LinkedIn advice, and introduced her to a web site designer, my daughter (whom you'll hear from later in this chapter).

By the time I got off that plane, I felt great. I'd offered help and enjoyed my endorphin rush. I'd made a new potential business friend. And the experience gave me the opportunity to reconnect with an old pal from high school. That's how the however-I-can-help approach should work: you don't feel like you're being sucked dry by helping others; you feel energized and exhilarated!

Genuine Connections Take Time to Build

At its core, Karmic Selling is just about connecting with people. Sometimes that means connecting people with others who can help them better than you can. A colleague of mine recently told me, "Stan, you match more people than a dating service." And it's true: I love connecting people when I sense that they might both find value in meeting each other. I'm always building my own circle. I also like to help other people build theirs.

Now, that circle of people doesn't get built overnight. You've got to put in the time. You've got to deliver results. If you promise an outcome, you've got to deliver on it. That means incorporating all the steps I've mentioned before this chapter, from preparing for meetings to following up. And it means *sticking with it*. Stick with people. Give them time to realize, "Hey, this person is for real. They really *do* want to help." Remember, our instinct is to be defensive—to cross those arms. You've got to persist past that point.

Even after you land a sale, remember that it's just the beginning of the relationship. You need to continue to do what you said you're going to do. It's not always easy to maintain that however-I-can-help mindset—I've struggled with it myself. But if you stick with it, it pays off big time—and you find yourself wanting to live life in this positive, authentic way both professionally and personally. You'll find that it makes you feel good. And you'll find that it brings you success.

I've found success through Karmic Selling largely because I've stuck with it. Through the moments of doubt, I've remained persistent—and the time and effort I've put in have resulted in lasting relationships. Today, I'm proud to say that 85 percent of The Kormac Group's revenue comes from client partners that we have worked with repeatedly over many years.

The best part is that I am now lucky enough to call some of those business friends personal friends. They've become members of my circle. That's what happened to me with Rich Tajer.

CASE STUDY

Rich Tajer (Enterprise Chief Commercial Officer & President Electrical Systems, Commercial Vehicle Group, Inc.)

I first met Rich in 2012, and we've kept in touch over the years. I think through 2016, we probably had upward of fifteen meetings. It wasn't until July 2016 that we signed a deal. Now, it was great to get that business. But more significantly, over the course of those years and those various meetings, Rich and I developed a relationship outside of business. Today, I consider him a personal friend.

When I met Stan, I noticed he had a different approach, which was very similar to my own—it was all about listening instead of trying to push a solution or product on somebody. So, I took note of that, and we kept in contact over the years, as both of us shifted through different roles and companies. Eventually, he helped me out with some product development processes and, later, with a major plant efficiency project. So, we've had a few professional engagements. But we've also developed a friendship. I talk to Stan about a lot of things unrelated to business, and we both bounce ideas off each other. I appreciate his insights because I know he shares my mindset of not forcing business and instead actually helping solve customer problems. He doesn't wedge himself in but offers ideas for how he can help, and if he can't help, he's upfront about that too.

Especially when dealing with consultants, you come to learn when people are being disingenuous. Integrity is important to me. I don't like to play games—I don't have time for them. Stan recognizes that. So, what started as a business relationship turned into a friendship. Like Stan, I believe that if you put good things out in the world, good things will happen. When you're helping somebody solve a problem, good things end up happening for you, too.

Rich is a great example of how a business friend can become a personal friend. In other cases, I've had business friends become valuable colleagues. That's what happened with Channing Rollo, a marketing powerhouse I'd met years back—who has now joined The Kormac Group.

CASE STUDY

Channing Rollo (Managing Director, The Kormac Group)

Channing has served in leadership positions at four international consultancies, an advertising agency, and a Fortune 500 utility. In 2008, she was recognized by Consulting Magazine *with a Women Leaders in Consulting Award. Needless to say, when Channing agreed to work for Kormac, I was thrilled—and floored.*

No one wants to work with jerks. Unfortunately, management consulting is rife with them. For over twenty years, I worked with and for a lot of clowns, requiring Herculean levels of grit. To survive in consulting's combative and competitive environment, I regret that I sometimes behaved like a jerk as well.

When I'd had my fill of toxicity, I took a sabbatical to raise my son and support my husband in the launch of his medical practice. But after a few years, I missed the challenge and collaboration of consulting. I reached out to a handful of folks I trusted, and Stan was at the top of my list.

My professional network is spread across more than a dozen consultancies, but I joined Stan at Kormac because he described it as "good people doing good work for good companies." He wasn't bluffing—I appreciated Kormac's no-asshole recruitment policy and commitment to delivering big results with small, expert teams. I started working with Kormac as a contractor but soon fell in love with its supportive, collegial environment.

After several years of collaboration, I asked to join Kormac's leadership team and share in its commitment to cultivating a heart-led organization. While my expertise is sales and marketing, we've grown largely through word of mouth because we genuinely care about our clients and each other. There's no better pitch than this: we are committed to shared success.

How to Create Your Own Circle

Rich and Channing are two great examples of how a however-I-can-help mindset allows you to surround yourself with awesome people. I'm proud to say they're part of my trusted circle of friends. However, not every relationship goes this route.

Over the years, I've realized that not everyone will accept the however-I-can-help mindset. Not everyone will believe you are being authentic in your clean-heart approach. They might feel like it's some kind of scam, or they might try to take advantage of your good intentions and scam *you*. The people who don't buy into the clean-heart approach probably aren't people you want to surround yourself with anyway. By practicing a clean heart, you'll weed out the people you don't want around.

As for how to build your own circle—the answers are all in this book. Go back to chapter 1, and check out that clean-heart checklist. Consider how you might use it in your business *and* your personal life. I won't call it a formula for success because I don't

Bringing a clean heart to life leads to a happier, less stressful, more authentic existence. And isn't that what we all want?

believe in magic pixie dust. Even if you practice all those steps, you won't get it right every time. I sure don't. I'm always trying new things, looking for new ways to connect, and considering what could have been done differently if a connection doesn't pan out. But I've found that, for the most part, bringing a clean heart to life leads to a happier, less stressful, more authentic existence. And isn't that what we all want?

I was pushing forty before I realized that the f— you chip and the asshole approach wasn't fulfilling for me. It took a car accident for me to get out of the corporate rat race. I'm proud to say that my daughter figured it all out a lot earlier—and without the need of a life-threatening accident. Let me introduce you to Ayla Gwizdak.

CASE STUDY
Ayla Gwizdak (Owner, Carpe Noctem Websites)

Ayla knew early on that the corporate world wasn't for her—so she started her own business. She's still in her twenties and she's already running the show (I guess you can tell that I'm a pretty proud dad). I can't take credit for her work, but I do like to think that my own journey inspired her.

I was probably about ten years old when my dad left his job. I remember him complaining about the long hours and the constant travel, and how he hated being away from the family. But I also remember him really struggling to decide whether he wanted to start his own thing. I remember him being very nervous about that. Eventually, he went for it. I didn't really think much of it at the time. I mean, you're a kid, right? So you barely know what your parents do. I'd tell people my dad was a business consultant, without really knowing what that meant, and they'd be like "Oh, cool," and that would be it.

As a web developer and designer, I began to empathize with my dad's complaints about his job as I found myself handling many business-related tasks in addition to my regular workload. This made me consider starting my own business, despite my initial nervousness. With the guidance of my dad, I took the leap and went back to college to gain the knowledge and skills needed to start my own business. I then landed my first client, which gave me the confidence to continue as a business owner. Today, I am proud of my accomplishments.

Are You Happy with Your Circle?

As we conclude this book, I want you to ask yourself: "Am I happy with my circle?" Consider it as this chapter's reflection exercise. If the answer is no, then you know it's time for a change. The clean-heart approach may be the answer. It's certainly helped me. And I'm hoping it'll help you, too.

Positive karma does come back. Sometimes it takes a while. You may have moments of doubt like I did. But often, when you're at your lowest, karma will come around the corner with the calvary to save you. If you lead your life authentically and approach others with a clean heart, I think you'll find that to be true. In the process, you'll find the people you can trust—and weed out those you can't. You'll build a circle of business partners, friends, family, and clients whom you can rely on and confide in. In my book, that's worth more than any sales deal.

*"Success is never owned. It's rented,
and the rent is due every day."*

—**RORY VADEN,** author and entrepreneur

CONCLUSION

When I started this book, it was meant to be about my sales approach. In the process of writing it, it turned into something more than that—because I came to realize that Karmic Selling isn't even *about* selling. It's simply about doing good. Now, we're not talking rocket science here. This isn't a new concept. You've probably seen it before in other forms, like "treat others as you want to be treated." But I think it's a reminder we could all use, and I've got the experience (and proof) to know that, when you put good out into the world, it really does come back tenfold.

I hope you don't need a major car wreck to shake you silly like I did. I hope this book can help you see the value in living authentically and with a clean heart. I don't care if this book sells millions of copies. If I can help my readers, that's good enough for me. And if one person tells me, "Stan, I read your book and improved my approach, and it changed my life for the better"—well, that would be freaking awesome.

If you want to see what value Karmic Selling can bring to your life, reach out to me—I will gladly help you. I'm constantly evolving my philosophy and widening my circle. You can check out the latest on my website, KarmicSelling.com, where I'm always adding ideas and material, from worksheets to checklists. You can also find my contact information there. **Let's connect. I want to know: How can I help you?**

To Everyone that made Karmic
Selling possible, thank you from
the bottom of my heart. I am
glad you are part of my life.
Forever Grateful!!!

STAN

ACKNOWLEDGMENTS

I'm profoundly grateful to everyone who contributed to the creation of this book. Their support, encouragement, pushing, pulling, and contributions made *Karmic Selling* possible.

First and foremost, I am indebted to my family for their unwavering support throughout this journey. Their love, understanding, patience, and input have been invaluable. Sandy, my wife, pulled me off the ledge several times as I went into each chapter thinking, "I have nothing to contribute to this chapter! I have no anecdotes, quotes that hit the point, nor do I have anyone I've met in my life who can support this chapter's message." Thank you, Sandy, for your steadfast guidance and encouragement! Thank you, Ayla, my older daughter, for sharing your story in chapter 10. I am so proud of you! Thank you, Anya, my younger daughter, for helping me to see life in a different way and pushing me to be a better person. You have a beautiful soul, and I am so proud of you!

I would like to thank many of my friends and colleagues who agreed to be featured in print to help me communicate this book's key messages, including Mike Smith, Mike Harris, John Weiss, Kelly Short, Jeff Lindow, Curt Howell, Millissa Flanagan, Rich Holder, Sarah Kirby, Marie Kelly, Dave Antis Jr., Kevin Nelson, Rich Tajer,

Channing Rollo, Ayla Gwizdak, and others whose stories appear in this book but are unnamed.

I am deeply humbled to work with an amazing team. To my circle at The Kormac Group, I love you all, and I thank you for reading each section of the book and providing me constructive feedback as it progressed. Thanks to all of you: Mike Borucke, Mike Harris, Channing Rollo, and Jeff Lindow. I want to specifically highlight Channing's guidance and help along the way: during the final stages of development, she and I read the book aloud to each other like we were back in kindergarten storytime. We made many edits to ensure a better book for our readers.

I'm also grateful to all the busy executives, friends, and family who took the time to read this book and provide thoughtful feedback. I'm honored by those who also provided a formal testimonial for this book, especially the friend who teared up as he shared what this book meant to him. Thank you Richard Ward, Kevin Wells, Bruce Hoechner, Steve Henderson, Steve Lazar, Paul Tudor, George Williams, Patrick Hastings, Marly Q Casanova, Boudewijn van Lent, Giuseppe Muzzi, and Wayne Lucernoni. Many times, I was moved to tears when I read your testimonials. I am so glad the *Karmic Selling* message resonated with you and you agreed to appear in this book. Thank you to the many unnamed contributors, as I had a timeline to meet in getting this into print. If I missed you, it's because of publication deadlines. I love you, and your messages about how this book touched you are all the success I need.

I appreciate my outstanding team at Forbes Books/Advantage Media for their professionalism, dedication, and belief in this book. Your expertise and commitment to excellence are inspiring. I want to highlight two folks specifically as they went above and beyond my expectations in writing this first book. I had the best ghostwriter ever in Alison Kilian. Her partnership made this book engaging and enjoyable to read. I am forever grateful and forever your friend, Alison. Also, thank you Joel Schettler for providing outstanding editing of this book and even letting me know, "I learned by reading this book; I believe you have something special here, Stan." Joel, I also consider you my friend, and I will help you any time you need it.

I am indebted to the numerous researchers, scholars, and experts whose work is referenced in this book. Their insights enriched the content. Also, thank you to those whose quotes are mentioned. Thank you for acting with kindness and understanding the power of karma. Your words resonated with me.

I would also like to acknowledge the reviewers and editors at the Forbes Books/Advantage Media team who have meticulously reviewed and improved my manuscript. Your attention to detail and commitment to ensuring the clarity of this book are deeply appreciated.

Thank you to everyone who showed me kindness over the years. For many of you, I can remember the exact experiences, and they still warm my heart. Because of you, I learned how to live a meaningful life of connection and service to others.

To all those named and unnamed who have provided their support and encouragement, I offer my heartfelt thanks. Your contributions have played an integral role in the completion of this book, and I am grateful for your presence in my life.

With love and gratitude,

Stan